Action Research and Reflective Practice

The use of reflection as a tool to support and develop practice is becoming increasingly recognised across education, health care and the social sciences. Reflection is used to create depth of knowledge and meaning, both for self and for those practised upon. Running alongside the use of reflection is the prevalent use of action research, which some see as a way of approaching the study of human beings from a philosophical perspective, in which sharing takes place within mutually supportive environments. As a result, many academics and practitioners suggest that one cannot improve the methodology of action research without considering philosophical reflection.

In *Action Research and Reflective Practice*, Paul McIntosh argues that reflective practice and action research can become mechanistic in their use unless fresh creative approaches are employed. Exploring the tension between the use of evidence-based practice, based upon solid 'objective' research, and reflection, with its 'subjectivity' and personal perception, this book argues that reflection is research. McIntosh increases the prevalence and effectiveness of both action research and reflection through the application of new creative and visual approaches.

Action Research and Reflective Practice demonstrates that creative approaches can be utilised effectively in critically reflexive ways, creating a new style of action research that is both innovative and theoretically robust. The resulting approach will improve evidence-based research in education, health care and other social sciences to enhance perception and understanding of events, identity and self. This book will be highly beneficial to undergraduate and postgraduate students, as well as educational and social researchers, across a broad range of subjects within the social sciences.

Paul McIntosh has a background of working as a practitioner in both health and social care in the field of learning disabilities, and extensive experience of higher education for health and social care professionals.

Action Research and Reflective Practice

Creative and visual methods to facilitate reflection and learning

Paul McIntosh

Routledge
Taylor & Francis Group

LONDON AND NEW YORK

First published 2010
by Routledge
2 Park Square, Milton Park, Abingdon, Oxon, OX14 4RN

Simultaneously published in the USA and Canada
by Routledge
270 Madison Avenue, New York, NY 10016

Routledge is an imprint of the Taylor & Francis Group, an informa business

© 2010 Paul McIntosh

Typeset in Galliard by
Keystroke, Tettenhall, Wolverhampton
Printed and bound in Great Britain by
TJ International Ltd, Padstow, Cornwall

British Library Cataloguing in Publication Data
A catalogue record for this book is available from the British Library

Library of Congress Cataloging-in-Publication Data
McIntosh, Paul.
Action research and reflective practice : creative and visual methods to
facilitate reflection and learning / Paul McIntosh.
p. cm.
1. Action research in education—Great Britain. 2. Reflective teaching—Great
Britain. I. Title.
LB1028.24.M386 2010
370.7'2—dc22   2009030417

ISBN10: 0–415–46901–5 (hbk)
ISBN10: 0–415–46902–3 (pbk)
ISBN10: 0–203–86011–X (ebk)

ISBN13: 978–0–415–46901–2 (hbk)
ISBN13: 978–0–415–46902–9 (pbk)
ISBN13: 978–0–203–86011–3 (ebk)

Contents

Acknowledgements

Although this book is entirely of my own construction, there are numerous people whose ideas have contributed to it. Not least Jack Sanger, whose guidance through the research itself and since has been invaluable. I also need to thank the teaching staff who have contributed to the reflective learning work that I have implemented within the Faculty of Health, Wellbeing and Science at University Campus, Suffolk, and have been prepared to take risks with their teaching in an ever-increasing conformist world of practice, in particular Jane Parr and Pauline Newson, and Catherine Theodosius for her critical readership.

Then there are the colleagues who have subsequently become friends: Paula Sobiechowska, whose wonderfully witty emails and conversations keep me sane; Jill Robinson, for always providing me with belief in myself and my work; and Angie Titchen, who has shown a true interest in what I am trying to do. I'm always flattered when Angie says, 'Thank you for thinking of me,' as I always feel it should be the other way round . . .

Finally, I have to thank the students who have participated so actively in my form of reflective learning and given such positive feedback. In particular, I wish to thank 'those who cannot be named' (though I wish I could, out of courtesy and respect) – those who have allowed me to use their work for this book – I am indebted to you, so thank you.

On a more personal note, I need to thank the nursing and medical team in West Bergholt Ward at Colchester General Hospital, who in 2007 quite literally put me back together, and the physiotherapy unit at Walnut Tree Hospital in Sudbury, Suffolk – Pat Large and Roy Lowhan – for getting me mobile again. I also need to thank Philip Mudd, my commissioning editor at Routledge, who has been so very patient and supportive in giving me the time I need to complete this book. And very last but not least, my wife Iona and daughters Romy and Brenna for all their care when I really needed it and since. Thank you.

Preface

In September 2007 I was involved in a serious road accident, which left me with three fractured thoracic vertebrae (amongst other fractures), severe head trauma, a collapsed lung and severe nerve damage to my upper right arm and shoulder. I spent a total of eight weeks in West Bergholt Ward at Colchester General Hospital in the UK, seven of them lying flat on my back. During that time – and since then – I have had such close contact with people in the health service that my friend and mentor Jack Sanger has suggested that the measures I took to conduct an ethnographic study of the NHS were, in hindsight, rather extreme! There is, however, a perverse truth to this joke, for I was able to witness first-hand the working lives of the medical and nursing staff, listen to their experiences and take part in the systems in which they function.

But first a word of praise: the care I have received throughout my recovery has been excellent, from my hospital admission through to discharge and ongoing therapy, and it is a testament to all those involved that I am back on my feet again. I owe them my gratitude for this. What concerns and puzzles me – and I see this book as something of a puzzle to be assembled – are the conflicts that these people work through as health professionals, and which I feel are shared by those working in the social and educational professions. First, there is the requirement for practice to be evidence-based through research, and by this I mean particular types of research which are grounded in scientific methodologies and used pragmatically; and second, there is the requirement to reflect upon one's own practice and to develop meaning from this, which creates understanding of oneself and of the person practised upon. Whilst I am fortunate that those who cared for me were certainly applying the principles of the former, my observations have led me to conclude that there is little, if any, engagement with the latter. This is not a criticism of those individuals; it is simply an observation of the efficiency model used in the NHS which is reliant on tangible productivity and output, and which leaves little opportunity, time or consideration for observations on ✓ the inner and outer world experienced by those who work within it.

Continuing with this theme of reductionism is the way in which reflective practice, when in use, is applied. The use of reflective practice as a tool to support and develop practice is becoming increasingly recognised across the health and social sciences and education. Reflection is assumed to create depth of knowledge and meaning for both the self and those practised upon, and its basis lies in self-awareness and awareness of others. It is also reliant on observation of both our inner and outer selves, and on the observation of ourselves by others. Yet we reduce this complex activity to a pragmatic and cyclical process, with subheadings and action plans that have limited use as a theoretical resource, but provide a reader with 'evidence' of 'reflection' produced by the writer. The articulation of any of this awareness is generally through language, and as professionals we are prone to limiting these observations in factual, objective and written text, for that is what counts as a professional standard. In short, we are losing the powers of creativity and intellectual-isation and have mislaid our reflexive roots in favour of all that is literal. It could be therefore argued that in its current misuse, reflection is not working.

It is at this juncture that I reinforce the point that the professional domain is governed by the judicious use of scientific evidence, and follow it by asking a question which in this case is applied to those working in the caring and education professions: *what is it, then, that makes this evidence work when it is applied to unique human beings?* This is something that I hope will become clear, and that will lead us to better understanding later.

At this point we come to action research. Some writers, such as John Elliott and Alison Morton-Cooper, feel that action research as a methodology cannot be improved upon unless the approach to it is *critically reflexive* (and I agree with them). In their view, claims to validity of knowledge within a particular domain can be examined and contested, leading to new ways of thinking, seeing and acting. What Donald Schon and others term 'reflective practice', Elliott (1991) terms 'action research', and I feel that the capacity for each of us to become individual *practitioner-researchers* lies in this concept.

This book is split into two halves, Part 1 and Part 2. In Part 1, Chapter 1 examines the tensions between evidence-based practice and reflective practice and draws upon a short history of medicine to illustrate the source of the model for evidence-based practice and the anomalies that exist within it; Chapter 2 explores the connections between reflection, action research and reflexivity, while Chapter 3 explores theories around consciousness and unconscious thinking as an exploration of how the mind 'reflects'. Part 2 focuses much more explicitly on the concept of creativity as a reflective and methodological tool, exploring methods for creativity as a form of action research. Chapter 4 discusses what I mean by creativity and introduces illustrations of creative work; Chapter 5 examines ways in which constructs of metaphor, symbolism and dialogics can be applied to creative methods; and Chapter 6 proposes a conceptual framework which opens up infinite possibilities of knowing and transformation through the application of creativity to action research and reflection. Chapter 7 concludes the book by concentrating on the fields of action research and critical creativity with a view to establishing the ways in which the principles and values of action research can be applied through creativity and how the outcomes of this may constitute evidence that is as 'real' as that of a positivist nature.

I have deliberately constructed the book so that Part 1 acts as a foundation for Part 2, inasmuch as it is a more descriptive representation of a range of theoretical approaches that can be seen collectively as factors influencing the current thinking on positivism, and the ways in which the mind can be understood as both a positivist and an interpretivist phenomenon. Laying this foundation is vital to enable a better appreciation and understanding of Part 2. In this sense each chapter is discrete and can be dipped into individually, but also plays a part in the structure of the book as a whole.

As such, what I plan to do in this book is progress from a 'hard science' point of origin and arrive at an end-point through each discrete chapter which culminates in a synthesis of the concepts of reflection and action research through the use of literary and visual art forms to enhance perception and understanding of events, identity and self, and their potential for teaching, learning and research methodology within the fields of health and social care, the social sciences and education. I use empirical data collected from postgraduate students involved in my own research and teaching practice and an eclectic range of theoretical ideas which guide the reader to become a 'creative practitioner-researcher'. I hope that what is gained from it are differing uses for differing roles, but essential to all of this is the use of creativity and creative media applied in different ways. For those looking to find new ways to reflect on their practice and their approach to it, you will find exciting and 'live' examples of these. For those looking to develop ways in which critical incidents can be explored through means other than written language, there are models that can be drawn upon and adapted. And for social scientists who are interested in the problems and benefits that visual data can bring to analysis and representation, there are theoretical ideas, methodologies and ways of analysing that will be useful. Ultimately I hope to lead us to the construction of a domain of action research, reflection and critical creativity, and I hope that the second half of the book will appeal to those in the growing fields of visual sociology and ethnography as much as to those involved in the caring professions, for as Emmison and Smith (2002: 2) have noted, 'the systematic use of visual data does not appear to figure prominently in the tool boxes of most empirically orientated social researchers'.

The body of literature in all the fields I discuss is huge, and it is impossible for me to encompass it all, so I have been pragmatic in its use. I have undoubtedly missed out some important literature, for which I apologise, but such omissions were inevitable, given the scale of this book.

The 'data' supplied in Part 2 is the product of a module which forms part of the postgraduate framework in the Faculty of Health, Wellbeing and Science at University Campus, Suffolk, called 'Reflexivity in Professional Practice'. In the assessment of this module, the students are asked to submit a 'creative portfolio' of their own making in any media of their choice: sculpture, music, film, paintings/drawings, poetry, stories, etc. The choices are in effect limitless.

Second, they are required to submit a reflective assignment based on the construction of the creative portfolio – a critical commentary on it – considering why they chose to represent what they did, why they presented it in such a way, and the kinds of theoretical models that underpinned their thinking. In effect, a reflection upon a reflection. The results of such work have been both diverse and startling in their quality, and have gone far beyond the means–end reasoning behind the assessed piece of work that was originally envisaged, and into a whole new domain of action research and critical creativity that is as highly welcome as it was unanticipated.

The data in Part 2 is by no means typical of the submissions: I simply made a pragmatic decision to include it, as some of the work cannot be accommodated in traditional book form. It does, however, provide an indication of what can emerge when engaging in such action.

References

Elliott, J. (1991) *Action Research for Educational Change*. Open University Press. Milton Keynes

Emmison, M. and Smith, P. (2002) *Researching the Visual*. Sage. London

Part I

From evidence-based practice to researcher of the self

Prelude

'Yes, that's right – look about you, you fool!' Breuer said to himself. 'People come from all over the world to see Venice – people who refuse to die before they are blessed by this beauty.'

How much of life have I missed, he wondered, simply by failing to look? Or by looking and not seeing? Yesterday he had taken a solitary walk around the island of Murano and, at an hour's end, had seen nothing, registered nothing. No images had transferred from his retina to his cortex.

(Yalom, 2005: 2)

This short extract from Irvin Yalom's *When Nietzsche Wept* is an illustration of the essence of what this book is about. It is to do with *really looking* and examining and exploring that which exists below the surface. What Yalom's character Breuer experiences is the realisation of an instrumentalist engagement with the world. One in which nothing other than the mechanics of living – in this case physiologically – matter for existence. It is for Breuer both frightening and intellectually illuminating, for he realises that this mode of living is easy to engage in yet lacking in substance. Once he has made this revelation to himself he is now in a position to change it.

These three chapters take an approach that first critiques the use of evidence-based practice as instrumentalist and which forces its users into mechanical ways of being as practitioners. In so doing, something is lost to their practice because what they see and experience is not transferred to their cortex. Second, it leads into ways in which experiences can be captured, noted, teased apart and reconstructed as deeper knowledge through personal insight and sharing. Through repositioning evidence-based practice as practice-based evidence, and by building on the concept that all practitioners can be researchers of their own practice through action research and reflective practices, I propose a move away from the use of pure instrumentalist practice and towards an approach that begins to develop a critique of its use. Third and finally, it is useful to explore the current and historical understanding of unconscious and conscious thought, both neuroscientifically and philosophically, so that we can begin to construct for ourselves an appreciation of behaviours, environments, experiences and physiology which impact on how we think and behave as 'practitioner-researchers' and on how we can apply best evidence reflexively.

Chapter 1

The tension in evidence-based practice and reflective practice

Then I decided to tell him a little story: The other day a man walked into the new dinosaur exhibit hall at the American Museum of Natural History in New York and saw a huge skeleton on display. He wanted to know how old it was, so he went up to an old curator sitting in the corner and said, 'I say old chap, how old are these dinosaur bones?'

The curator looked at the man and said, 'Oh, they're sixty million and three years old, sir.'

'Sixty million and three years old? I didn't know you could get that precise with ageing dinosaur bones. What do you mean sixty million and three years old?'

'Oh well,' he said, 'they gave me this job three years ago and at the time they told me they were sixty million years old.'

(Ramachandran, 2005: 18–19)

Introduction

There can be no doubt that in the modern world we are reliant on 'best evidence'. Governments act on the basis of what the science tells them – in the UK, for instance, the well-publicised responses to outbreaks of mad cow disease, foot and mouth disease and avian flu in the last ten years or so have all been relayed to the general public as the government acting on what the scientific evidence says. We see it in the way that medical practitioners are advised to prescribe medication on the basis of economy through a meta-analysis of clinical trials and surgical techniques, and we are now beginning to see it with regard to climate change and the ways in which energy needs can be best accommodated in the future. This fixation with best evidence has slowly but surely entered the various fields in which people work with other people. This may be direct work that helps those in need, such as health care, social care or education, or it may be indirect work, such as observing human beings and their interactions with the world in order that we may understand ourselves better, as in the social sciences.

I do not suggest that we should not work to what is considered at the time to be best evidence, for it clearly has an important place, but I would suggest that focusing so heavily on the ideal of best evidence through positivism is detrimental to wider notions of learning and understanding, particularly as there are only a limited number of research approaches which are considered to be scientifically 'sound'. We have even seen this in recent years in the UK higher education system, once a bastion of new knowledge and academic endeavour, whereby universities have been scrutinised through the Research Assessment Exercise and any published works are subject to, and only considered valid if they are grounded in, scientific rigour. In short, the practice of recording what is observable and narrow is prioritised over more theoretical work that could open up a field of inquiry rather than close it down. The field of health care, more so than social care or education, has historically wrestled with the issues in the debate on *art versus science*, but the question is now spreading into these other domains too.

Now I shall review this debate and examine it in the relatively recent light of *evidence-based practice* and *reflection*, which I believe effectively replaces the *arts versus science* terminology. Evidence-based practice is a term and a practice commonly used in health and social care. It is possibly less well known in the field of education, but nonetheless the principles remain the same: essentially it is used to perceive a problem, seek out the most valid research evidence to address that problem, and then apply it to the problem, the results of which can be measured as to their efficacy. In essence, this approach is distinctly different to experiential learning, which is viewed currently as subjective and difficult to measure accurately. However, the nature of research and evidence is open to constant debate and contest. Initially, I would like to provide a small vignette on the development of evidence-based medicine and the conflicts which have existed (and still do exist) about what is valid. From this I will broaden the discussion into one of evidence-based practice, experiential learning and reflection more generally.

The roots of evidence-based practice – a very brief history of medicine

The basis of what we now understand broadly as evidence-based practice has at its heart the role of evidence in medicine – first in determining it as a profession with unique knowledge and power (see Illich, 1977, which is as valid today as it was then), and second as a way in which interventions can be known to be effective and standardised. Whilst the construct of evidence-based medicine might be relatively new, the use of evidence-based intervention is not, and it is the correlation between cause and effect that has been sought and illustrated since man first documented his existence.

As long as we have existed we have desired – *needed*, perhaps – to make connections between natural phenomena and to use them for our wellbeing. Although theories have changed across a wide expanse of time and geography, they form part of the continuum of the use of evidence to secure our longevity. The understanding of correlations and causations between the universe and illness may have been different – for instance, Inglis (1965) writes of the relationships ascribed to illness and cosmic phenomena in the ancient civilisation of Babylonia. Today, we know that weather can affect such conditions as asthma and seasonal affective disorder, and this may have comprised evidence for the Babylonians. Inglis (1965) also notes that the Babylonians had a professional rule book for the practice of medicine: the Code of Hammurabi (1790 BC), which existed to protect citizens rather than to provide any peace of mind for the practitioner, and could have brutal consequences for those who got their intervention wrong.

If a physician shall make a severe wound with a bronze operating knife on the slave of a free man and kill him, he shall replace the slave with another slave.

If a physician shall make a severe wound with an operating knife and kill him . . . his hands shall be cut off.

(Extract from the Code of Hammurabi, quoted in Inglis, 1965: 16)

Roy Porter (1996) confirms that fees paid to a healer were specified on a sliding scale, depending on the status of the patient, and that draconian measures similar to those imposed on incompetent shipwrights and architects were implemented for failure.

This form of regulation – although not quite so punitive in the twenty-first century AD – is not dissimilar to that which exists today, for it places responsibility on the practitioner to know what he is doing through what is known. In the modern day this is enshrined legally, for only those who are appropriately trained and qualified are able to diagnose, prescribe and treat. There are other similarities with the past, too. Porter (1996) recognises that competing healers in Greek society, such as bone-setters, surgeons, physicians and exorcists, formed a market place from which choices of treatment were left to individual patients to decide, but that this market existed within a set of rules for medical ethics and advertising, much in the way that today a governmental rhetoric of 'choice' is espoused as policy. Arguably this principle applies to the wider delivery of health and social care through the 'care management' process, in which local authorities assess, plan and cost care needs, then turn to the market place for tender. The care provider who appears to deliver the best value for money is then funded and regulated. However, the representatives of the state now decide, not the individuals in need of care. As well as these market place approaches to health and social care, in the UK changes are taking place in compulsory education through the development of foundation schools – a new form of school governance designed to create competition through the guise of quality improvement.

The early Greek understanding of medicine was similar to that of the Babylonians, relying mainly on cosmic or mythical interventions for cure, but it was transformed in its later period by the introduction of rationality and systematics to Greek thought. Hippocrates has long been attributed with leading this transformation in medicine by using a systematic approach based on observation, comparison and recording of disease – however, it is probably wrong to suggest that Hippocrates himself was responsible for this, as it is likely that the scientific nature of Greek thought meant that he was but one of many involved in this process; arguably, as Inglis (1965) suggests, he may simply have been in the right place at the right time. Two main forms of medicine existed during this period: *allopathy* – a doctrine of contraries; and *homeopathy* – a doctrine of similars. In their simplest forms, these approaches could be easily divided. Allopathy suggested that to confront a symptom with something that restored a balance was the correct course of action: so, to reduce a fever, the patient must be cooled down; similarly, a constipated patient must be given a laxative. Homeopathy, suggested through Hippocratic teaching, was grounded in the notion that each person had a life force – a protective entity that acted to safeguard the individual. In this view the life force could act to prevent the possibility of disease – for instance, vomiting or the formation of boils as symptomatic of disease was not necessarily due to the disease itself, but to ward it off. In this case, rather than preventing a symptom such as vomiting – as allopathy would prescribe – the purpose of the intervention would be to assist the life force by encouraging the vomiting in order to throw off the disease or poison. Although these doctrines existed as separate sects, it was inevitable that physicians would come to use them interchangeably, based on their observations of outcomes, and in this we begin to see the birth of empiricism, but not as we now know it.

The first to bring these differing approaches together was Galen, born in the ancient Greek city of Pergamum, who spent the majority of his medical life attending to emperors in Rome during two periods totalling over thirty years. Galen was renowned for his ability to diagnose and treat, but he was also a keen recorder of his work and findings as well as a perceptive anatomist, and he strongly advocated placing anatomy as central to medicine, rather than cosmology or mythology (Porter, 1996). Galen's approach made him useful to teachers and students of medicine. Inglis (1965) writes that Galen practised and preached a mixture of personal experiences and rival theories fused together in a somewhat unorthodox Pythagorean structure, for although it followed a rationalist process it did not quite add up, and would be distorted and oversimplified in order to appear coherent. He also used and exhorted the value of polypharmacy. As Inglis (1965: 38) notes, he wrote that 'It is the business of pharmacology to combine drugs in such a manner . . . as shall render them effective in combating or overcoming the conditions which exist in all the different diseases.' Of course, in reality this meant experimentation. If one drug did not work then another would be tried, or a different dosage, or a combination of drugs. Although the results of this practice were erratic, Galen believed that his methods were empirical. A point had been reached where some results were striking, but others were not. Medicine as a discipline was now formulating some theories about what works, but not how it works, and was still considered by many – including Galen himself, to an extent – to be linked to supernatural forces.

What followed were some first steps into medical orthodoxy – the truth – which were inclusive of all these factors. In terms of discovery and research, the Romans were keen anatomists. Physicians were limited in knowing how the body works by having access to it only in its deceased state. It would be far better, it was surmised, if it could be opened up and viewed whilst still living. Therefore, it was decreed that the live bodies of miscreants and deviants could be used for such experimentation, so physicians were able to open up their living bodies to view blood circulation, the mechanics of breathing, digestion and so on, and to record their findings. Those selected for this research would have been put to death anyway, so to die in agony in the cause of science was, to the Roman way of thinking, ethically sound.

Once the Roman Empire and its economic prosperity had vanished, the Dark and Middle Ages, and to some degree the Renaissance period, were limited in progressing medicine. Few new texts were written, and what did exist was reduced to handbook form from the original learned texts. There were, however, some pockets of progression, such as that in Salerno in Italy, a vibrant medical community that was well placed to derive knowledge from the Greek and Arab worlds which reintroduced theoretical speculation and medicine as an academic study and practice based loosely on a model of Galenism (Porter, 1996). And although the anatomical drawings of Leonardo da Vinci and Visalius went some way to disproving many of Galen's theories concerning the operation of the internal organs and blood system, the Middle Ages are renowned for reversing medical practice and thought. So, making a rather large leap, both temporally and historically, we arrive at the seventeenth century.

This period can be generally characterised by its increasing stress on the use of science. Although actual advancements in medicine were few, it was an era when tools, such as microscopes, became more technologically developed. Rationality in science and rationality as an approach to medicine through the use of science became the cornerstones of research across northern Europe. The issues of allopathy and homeopathy encountered in the Hippocratic period still remained as conflicting approaches to medicine, despite increasing scientific endeavour. For instance, the physician Thomas Sydenham was opposed to the dominant doctrine of the contraries and the use of polypharmacy, suggesting, in an extension of the doctrine of similars, that symptoms were not the effect of the disease, but of the body's struggle to overcome it. Furthermore, he suggested that certain diseases were particles disseminated in the atmosphere which entered the body, mixed with the blood and were carried throughout the entire organism as entities. Though similar in some ways to the Hippocratic belief that symptoms were a sign of the 'life force' at work, Sydenham's ideas were more organically grounded, suggesting observation of symptoms rather than theory in clinical medicine, and that there were specific diseases which required specific remedies (Porter, 1996). But medical orthodoxy at the time favoured allopathy, so Sydenham's ideas fell into disrepute until after his death, when generations of doctors returned to the laboratory to try to find the cause of disease entities that he had accurately described.

By the mid-1700s the rationalist hold had begun to take two forms which continued to develop the concepts of allopathy and homeopathy. These became known as the Iatrophysical and Iatrochemical schools. Iatrochemists followed the notion of the 'life force', believing that failure of an aspect of the life force due to disease would show itself as a chemical change of body tissue, usually in one organ, and the treatment was to provide a chemical response directed at the organ concerned. One man, Jan van Helmont, began to develop a field of research into chemistry, for instance discovering carbonic acid, while his compatriot Franz de la Boe preached simplistic approaches, such as the use of acids to counteract excesses of alkali. But the inevitable criticism of such medicine remained the same: that they did not know the causes of what they were attempting to treat; and that any remedies could be found only by testing, trial and error. As such, their successes were limited.

The Iatrophysicist view was more one of engineering: taking more of a Cartesian view, they saw the body as a machine, so, if they were able to understand its mechanics then the disease would be understood, too. Underpinning this idea was a mathematical attitude through the use of logic. The man attributed with bringing the ideas of Iatrophysics to mainstream Europe, Hermann Boerhaave, stated: 'Every vital action depends on certain bodily conditions and relations; every change in these bodily conditions and relations is necessarily followed by a corresponding change in the vital activity; medicine, therefore, must be based on physiology' (cited in Inglis, 1965: 108).

Boerhaave's notions, developed in the early eighteenth century, became dominant in medicine in the twentieth century: they suggested that in treating the physical end-product of the disease, one was then able to treat the disease itself. Boerhaave was renowned for his diligence as a physician and for sound clinical judgement. He recorded a patient's case history with meticulous care; diagnosis and prognosis followed; and finally there was advice on treatment. His was a scientific spirit of medicine, which dealt little in abstraction.

Alongside these debates came the development of preventative medicine. In the seventeenth century smallpox was rife amongst all classes in Europe, and it was fatal in roughly 25 per cent of cases. The process of inoculation against the disease was already known in the Far East, reaching Europe through Turkey. This was well-established practice, and included ways in which the strains of disease could be made less virulent and the risks of inoculation therefore diminished. In England the most famous example of smallpox inoculation was through the practice of the country physician Edward Jenner. He took a sample of cowpox from a young girl, transferred it into two young boys, then some days later injected the boys with smallpox germs. No ill effects were recorded. On the basis of this experiment, Jenner proclaimed himself a hero of modern medicine. The Royal Society of Medicine rejected his findings as 'amateurish', which in truth they were, but this was due in the main to the rather unscientific method of discovery. Only later, when his theories were tested on a grand scale by the Austrian sanitary authorities and then by the United States Army, was Jenner rewarded.

This is not merely a historical fact. It gives an indication of the way in which current medical research and its evidence are grounded. Jenner's findings could not possibly form a truth in orthodox medical terms because his study was minutely small, but as the sample sizes grew so did the probability of success and therefore generalisation of that success. This epidemiological approach to medicine and public health is as true in the twenty-first century as it was in the seventeenth.

A pattern in the practice of medicine was beginning to emerge by the late eighteenth century – a case of two steps forward and one back. Although advances such as inoculation had been made, the ability to diagnose had not much improved since the Roman period, and indeed any diagnostic tools were often met with suspicion. The physician René Laennec began to use the art of auscultation – listening to the sounds of the organs, particularly the heart and lungs – as a diagnostic method, and it was in the conduct of his work on a girl with heart trouble that he came upon what has become the defining symbol of medicine. Reluctant to press his ear upon the chest of the girl for fear of acting inappropriately, he rolled up some paper and placed one end over the heart and the other to his ear. To his surprise, he heard the heart beating with greater clarity than if he had placed his ear directly upon her chest. The stethoscope was born. So it is to René Laennec that we owe the sight of doctors wandering the corridors of hospitals adorned with their statement of power and status draped decoratively around their shoulders.

Yet this development was not met with open arms by the profession at the time. Initially, the English College of Physicians sneered at the stethoscope. John Elliotson, who championed its introduction after seeing it in use on the continent, was asked, 'Ah, do you use that hocus pocus?' and told, 'You will learn nothing by it, and if you do, you cannot treat the disease better' (cited in Inglis, 1965: 127). Of course, we now know the stethoscope to be one of the greatest contributions to medicine as a diagnostic aid. But it was only after Laennec's death from tuberculosis –

the irony cannot go unnoticed, given the valuable assistance the stethoscope made to that disease's diagnosis – that it became an invaluable piece of the physician's equipment.

Moving on, it is difficult to be specific about what caused the revolution in medicine in the mid-nineteenth century, but amid the acrimonious infighting between physicians and surgeons about which treatments actually worked (therapy or the knife) a revolution *did* occur. Technically, the ability to discover what caused disease was improving, and as a result of major advances in microbiology by Louis Pasteur, from which came the development of sterile procedures during surgery using Joseph Lister's carbolic spray, mortality and morbidity levels began to fall. A Russian based in Pasteur's institute, Elie Metchnikoff, began watching cell behaviour under a microscope and saw how white blood cells moved into action when faced with an invasion from a virus. He realised that if the cells have experience of fighting the virus in measured doses, they are able to fight off further attacks. As a result of his findings, the practice of inoculation – or, as Pasteur termed it, 'vaccination' – began to be developed in systematic form. From this point forward, it was a process of establishing which diseases could be easily vaccinated against, and which were problematic.

The development of penicillin in the twentieth century reduced levels of mortality further, but such advances were not without their problems. Other drugs, such as insulin and cortisone, were developed alongside it, but, like penicillin, these were not subject to the rigorous forms of testing that exist today, and often led to morbid side-effects. Drugs were developed to counteract the effects of others, and by the 1960s polypharmacy, once ridiculed by the early physicians, was at its height.

At this point, I want to take a detour from this short history to explore one of the central tenets in how I problematise the issue of 'evidence'. The case of cortisone is interesting in relation to its usage and success, so I wish to focus on it for a while.

Cortisone, a hormone isolated in the 1930s, was used initially to treat rheumatoid arthritis. The results were spectacular: some arthritics lost stiffness and pain in their limbs; others, long bed-ridden, were suddenly able to get up and walk. Alongside these successes, however, were disturbing side-effects. As well as undesirable cosmetic changes, such as facial hair growth in women, disorders such as heart disease and stomach ulcers were reported, and patients were highly susceptible to some infectious disorders. In a study carried out by the British Medical Research Council comparing the benefits of cortisone with aspirin, the conclusion was that cortisone had 'not materially affected the prognosis' and that treatment with aspirin was often more likely to prove satisfactory than the use of cortisone. So why did cortisone appear to have such remarkable results when it was first introduced? Although the power of the drug itself cannot be ignored entirely, another factor was at work – the power of suggestion.

The placebo – a mock drug used to pacify those with hypochondriac tendencies – now became the centre of research attention (Inglis, 1965). Out of this attention came the practice of 'double blind' trials, where one group would be given a drug, and the other a placebo. Crucially, neither the administering doctor nor the patient knew who was getting what. The results were sometimes startling. Patients given placebos for common ailments such as colds, coughs, headaches and anxiety began to be relieved by their belief in the effects of the 'drug'. Up to a third of patients in studies reported by Dr Henry Beecher in 1955 expressed satisfaction and relief following the unknowing administration of a placebo. Without delving into the medical ethics of whether it is acceptable to prescribe a placebo to an unwitting patient, there is another matter at hand – a significant number of humans respond to the power of suggestion.

For some time, medicine had been trying to accumulate its knowledge and power through science, not by expounding theories of the super-natural, yet at this point it was confronted by processes which in effect could be seen no differently to the shamanism practised throughout the underdeveloped world.

Contextualising the history of medicine for current analysis

Two factors are apparent from this short overview of medical history: the systematic and narrow approach which medicine takes to establish new knowledge, and which sets aside the psychology of what it means to be human; and the way in which evidence is accessed and understood by those unfamiliar with how results are found. Furthermore we have seen that those physicians who have developed theoretical and practical approaches to medicine have constantly been at odds with each other as to what is the correct 'evidence' upon which to base a diagnosis and treatment, and this remains the same in modern-day practice. Medical science, which acts as the conduit to 'best evidence', is not immune to findings which are contradictory to each other or which raise other health alarms.

There is no doubt that evidence is based on numerical power. The Cochrane Collaboration, for instance, takes all studies conducted into fields of inquiry, sorts them into their replicated methodological approaches and then crunches together the results to increase the statistical significance and probability of the findings, thereby increasing their generalisability – a new form of truth and medical orthodoxy. Whilst this approach has some merit, and there may indeed be some generalisable principles in these findings, there is also a flaw: people are not generalisable and each will react differently to the same diagnosis and proposal for intervention.

The second point can have far-reaching consequences, so I want to explore this further. In 1998, a paper was published in the *Lancet* linking the single-vaccine jab for measles, mumps and rubella to autism. Although based on a small study which has since been called into question, the issue of single- or multiple-jab vaccines for the above diseases has now raged for ten years. The 1998 study received substantial media coverage, and although inconclusive scientifically because of its small sample size, its results have led to a plethora of research either to prove or disprove its findings, leading ultimately to a reduction in the take-up of immunisation using the triple vaccine for measles, mumps and rubella by parents anxious about its potential effects, with the inevitable consequence of a rise in the cases of these diseases in the UK and the USA. This original research based on a statistically small study group, utilising a methodology and data collection methods that have since been held up to medical and scientific scrutiny, has led to substantial concerns in public health, yet the debate on this issue continues.

From evidence-based medicine to evidence-based practice

> The proof of the pudding of evidence-based medicine lies in whether patients cared for in this fashion enjoy better health. This proof is no more achievable for the new paradigm than it is for the old, for no long-term randomized trials of traditional and evidence-based medical education are likely to be carried out.
>
> (Freshwater and Rolfe, 2004: 76–7)

Moving on from our potted medical history, in which huge chunks have been omitted in the name of expediency, we arrive at the current state of play. We have seen how rationalism, systematics and science have come to form the cutting edge of medical research and practice, and now it is time to examine what this means in reality.

So what exactly is evidence-based medicine in its current form? Sackett *et al.* (2001: 1) describe it as 'the integration of best research evidence with clinical expertise and patient values'. *Best research evidence*, they suggest, derives from patient-centred clinical research which focuses on the precision of diagnostic tests, the power of prognostic markers (i.e. recovery potential) and the safety and efficacy of therapeutic, rehabilitative and preventative measures. They also make the point that new research findings subsume those that are already established and replace them with those that are safer, more accurate, more efficacious, etc. *Clinical expertise* refers to the use of clinical skills and experience to identify health states, diagnosis, individual risks and benefits to potential interventions, and the personal values and expectations of patients. *Patient values* are the unique preferences and concerns of patients in the clinical experience which should be fundamental to clinical decision-making. As McWhinney (1995: 10) writes, 'Our first task is to recapture the capacity to respond to our patients prereflectively and spontaneously. As Kay Tombs (1992) put it, a patient wants to be recognized, appreciated and understood. This means responding to a patient's suffering.'

As a discipline of medicine, 'evidence-based practice' was named in 1992 by a group at McMaster University in Canada, and it has swiftly increased in international scope. There are now at least six journals dealing in EBM, in a number of languages, reaching a worldwide circulation of over 175,000. Its usage is therefore not in doubt, and it is the result of some very specific factors, as Sackett *et al.* (2001: 3) identify:

1   The development of strategies for effectively tracking down and appraising the evidence for its validity and relevance.
2   The creation of systematic reviews and concise summaries of the effects of health care (such as the Cochrane Collaboration).
3   The creation of evidence-based journals of secondary publication (those that publish 2% of clinical articles that are both valid and of immediate clinical use).
4   The creation of information systems for bringing the foregoing to us in seconds.
5   The identification and application of effective strategies for lifelong learning and for improving clinical performance.

I spoke earlier of how evidence-based medicine was becoming the new medical orthodoxy – a response to the use of outdated textbooks, frequently wrong expert decision-making, and ineffective education. Yet there is a caveat to this, for the new medical orthodoxy is not one based on 'truth'; it is one based upon constant change in knowledge. This is in line with what some philosophers and historians of science would call 'discontinuity' or 'rupture'. One philosopher of science, Georges Canguilhem, suggested that ultimately what we find from research is where we were wrong rather than where we were right. Drawing on the work of Gaston Bachelard, he states, 'The events of science are linked together in a steadily growing truth . . . At various moments in the history of thought the past of thought and experience can be seen in a new light' (Canguilhem, 1988: 11). He then (1988: 14) goes on to cite the work of Jean Cavailles on the nature of progress:

> One of the fundamental problems with the doctrine of science is precisely that progress is in no way comparable to increasing a given volume by adding a small additional amount to what is already there, the old subsisting with the new. Rather, it is perpetual revision, in which some things are eliminated and others elaborated. What comes after is greater than what went before, not because the present contains or supersedes the past but because the one necessarily emerges from the other, and in its content carries the mark of its superiority, which is in each case unique.

The 'best evidence' is therefore only ever fleeting, and in the world of science, as has always been the case, conflicting. New approaches, as Thomas Sydenham and John Elliotson found, are not always received with open arms, for we prefer, as Cavailles notes, our knowledge to be incremental and viewed through a narrow lens, even though that may mean throwing what we have believed to be right into the waste basket when we discover something new.

I do not wish to dwell on the nature of evidence-based medicine for too long, as its focus is ultimately too narrow for the purposes of this book. However, its principles do have some bearing on a later discussion, with regard to the asking of the right questions. In EBM this relates to a set of questions which not only leads to an appropriate diagnosis, but to a search for the appropriate literature and research, and the way in which that research has been conducted as to its validity in order to provide the most suitable intervention. EBM is also pivotal in the development of evidence-based practice, and we now enter this broader domain.

Liz Trinder (2001) notes that there has been an adoption of the key concepts of evidence-based medicine in a range of other disciplines and professions since the early 1990s under the overarching title of 'evidence-based practice'. This has occurred in most health fields, such as nursing, public health, dentistry, physiotherapy and mental health, and even into areas which have historically resisted what they consider a paternalistic approach to practice, including social work, education, probation and human resource management.

The main factor in the emergence of evidence-based practice is based centrally in the idea of the research–practice gap, which to some degree is different to the theory–practice gap, for it is concerned with the limited use of research findings that professionals use to guide their actions rather than that which is informed by theoretical ideas. In other words, we have historically relied on textbooks for knowledge and practice rather than more current research literature. Trinder (2001) suggests that less reliable resources have predominantly been used, such as knowledge gained during primary training, prejudice and opinion, outcomes of previous cases, advice from colleagues, and fads and fashions. In a sense, then, EBP is in practical terms a good idea, for it underpins all that is necessary for good professional practice. And yet it is fraught with challenges and flaws which make it difficult to operate and to work within. Trinder identifies two points which reflect these issues. First, there is the research itself – its quality, and the ability of those reading it to judge its quality and determine that correct judgement has been applied. And this itself is contentious, as Freshwater and Rolfe (2004: 81) point out, for the reading of such literature assumes that an accurate diagnosis has been made prior to searching the evidence, yet we know this is not always the case. Dawes *et al.* (2005) also suggest that, on average, clinicians are unable to answer four questions per surgery or clinic (Covell *et al.*, 1985), while Dawes and Uchechukwu (2003) say that most answers are found in printed sources. However, in observation, they appear to get them from their colleagues. Whether this knowledge is current or appraised with a degree of understanding is debatable.

The furore caused by the MMR/autism research discussed earlier is a well-known exemplar of a lack of appreciation of critical appraisal of the evidence, not only because it appears to be methodologically unsafe from a scientific or positivist perspective, but because it was embraced as truth by a significant number of people not *au fait* with research methodology. Although most professional education programmes now include research methods as a component of their provision, it is still fair to say that many professionals do not have a grasp of this, or a desire to engage in it through continuing professional development.

Trinder's (2001) second point concerns information (or, as Dawes (2005) calls it, clinical) overload. The volume of information and current research is such that it is virtually impossible to keep up to date with it. This, coupled with the speed at which it changes and at which it can be accessed, makes it difficult to digest, retain and recall. There is also a link to the first issue: rapid judgement has to be made about whether research is useful and rigorous, or weak or unreliable.

Given these issues, how has EBP managed to establish such an enduring foothold in our professional and non-professional lives? Trinder (2001) provides an excellent overview. She argues that EBP is a 'product of its time', and that there are tenets under which our lives are played out which are central to this. First, there is the notion of the 'risk society'. In this, the possibility of risk can be assessed and controlled by the knowledge of the professional and/or procedures put in place to minimise this. Remember the Code of Hammurabi that was discussed earlier – that there is an expectation of knowledge in order to practise? The modern practice of risk aversion is still grounded in those basic principles. Interestingly, though, Trinder notes a paradox in that although we are expected to be risk averse, and expect practices upon ourselves to be risk averse, we are actually more sceptical and mistrusting than our forebears because we are increasingly aware of the limitations of science and medicine and recognise that many modern problems are due to flawed scientific systems. Second, we are less likely to accept matters as they appear, because we understand the fluidity and constant revision of tradition and social practices. Third, our daily lives are filled with contradictory information and we subsequently develop a psychology where nothing is absolute. For instance, the turnaround of faith in the learned men of government and medicine in the last hundred years is startling. At the beginning of the twentieth century, the word of government or of medicine was taken as absolute. In the twenty-first century – practice and knowledge so much advanced to that of the early twentieth – our esteem in these professions has diminished and our expectations of them have changed. Risk assessment has become as much about protection of practitioners as it is about consideration of the safety of the people upon whom they practise.

Then there is the 'appliance of science'. For this, Trinder (2001) draws upon the work of Anthony Giddens (1991) and what he calls 'sustained optimism'. In this he sees a position where continued faith is placed in reason and science, and where there is a belief that we will still find solutions to major problems and the creation of security through rationalism, science and technology. What we see in evidence-based practice is an increased move to, and greater alignment with, science practising in ever more rigorous and scientific ways. This is also in part due to the notion of risk aversion. Trinder cites the work of Beck (1992) in his description of science shifting its position as a mechanism for social change to one of protection from harm in which risk assessment becomes central yet remains imperfect. This move from the confidence of scientific discovery to a cautious 'feeling of the way' in scientific progression is a more resistant form of science as it means it is less open to challenge. EBP, Trinder notes, takes this model and provides a methodology and procedures under which an evolving body of knowledge can be created, rather than one reliant on large theory.

Alongside the ways in which risk is managed is the influence of auditing and managerialism. Some primary changes in political ideologies and the devolution of government expenditures and accountabilities have formed discourses such as value for money, performance management, efficiency and effectiveness. Managerialism, Trinder (2001) notes when citing Clarke and Newman (1997), has been presented as a solution which can rise above political interference and professional power through objective rational, efficient and accountable decision-making in the use of resources. For instance, the NHS Executive in 1996 defined clinical effectiveness as: 'The extent to which specific clinical interventions when deployed in the field for a particular patient or population do what they are intended to do, that is, maintain and improve health and secure the greatest possible health gain from the available resources' (McSherry *et al.*, 2002: 5).

Following on from this has been the rise of the 'audit society', in which a heightened sense of risk has been coupled with a growing mistrust of expert judgement, with the result being less confidence in experts and more trust in audit systems. This moves the emphasis from the professionals to get things right and places it within systems of quality of expert services. Evidence-based practice is linked to this through the concepts of lifelong learning, as Trinder (2001: 67) identifies in the work of Michael Power (1997): 'The audit explosion is to do with the need to install a publicly auditable self-inspecting capacity with attempts to link ideals of accountability to those of self-learning.'

One of the inevitable consequences of such ideologies is a proceduralisation of practices. Establishing a distinct set of procedures through which a practice appears to work becomes the focus. Ultimately it is the procedure that becomes the dominant force, not necessarily the output, and in order for this to occur, the practice within the procedure needs to be observable and measurable to appear substantive. Alternative methodologies and ideas are excluded by the procedure so that it cannot be contaminated by the messiness and complexity of real-world phenomena, reducing information to bite-sized pieces that can be easily digested, yet not connected to the wider world.

Finally, Trinder (2001) discusses professionalism, empowerment and consumerism. In this discussion a paradox emerges, for even though evidence has constituted a significant component in the growth and power of managerialism – something which the professionals have resisted in their attempts to retain power and control – they now find themselves mirroring the procedures that have developed, such as auditing, in their approaches to evidence-based practice, in order that they can maintain an equal footing. Fundamentally, the emphasis on performance and effectiveness has not been isolated to management. A cultural shift has occurred in public services which has led to a greater transparency in how organisations and the professionals that work within them function, how money is spent, and levels of productivity. Now there is a degree of conflict between differing quality agendas – an agenda of organisational efficiency; and an agenda of professional value and user interests – yet both are applying the same methodological principles to establish an authoritative position. This battleground for supremacy is further muddied by one of the great political ideologies of the late twentieth century – consumer choice. Both of the above agendas are constructed towards particular outcomes – to find that which is most effective – which inevitably leads to a narrowing of possibilities and choices for those at the sharp end of managerial and professional decisions through their rigorous processes.

Ultimately, Trinder (2001) asks how the notions of incorporating patient wishes within clinical decision-making can be applied within such narrow systems of what is deemed to be the correct action advised through the available evidence. These issues are not unique to medicine: they can be found in almost every field, including education, social work, nursing and so on. Whether we are involved with service users, students or patients as contributors to consultation, improving our services through their experience becomes problematic, for ultimately the question of what is scientifically the best evidence will influence how service provision is configured. As a result there is a struggle to make service user/patient voices real and not just tokenistic acoustics to service provision. This has led to a conflation of differing types of practice which have become one entity. As Rolfe (2000) suggests, for those in nursing and the helping professions, evidence-based practice and research based practice have become synonymous with each other, yet these practices can and should be seen differently at a practical level, for different skills need to be applied for each, and we need to understand how inquiry can be conducted strategically and how to interpret its findings critically. However, there is also the nature of how we engage uniquely with our practice and what we derive from it personally as 'evidence'.

Practice-based evidence

Bearing in mind what is written above, I would like to ask a question: what makes an intervention work in order that some evidence is created? Below is a very simple scenario:

> A woman is the unfortunate victim of early-onset dementia. She is prescribed a particular drug that will maintain her current status, but due to her mental state she refuses to take it. Through the work of her care staff she eventually begins to take the drug and her current status is maintained.

So, we have something here which is very measurable. The drug is prescribed and taken and there is an outcome – our evidence. But something else has occurred – a practice which is more difficult to measure – the interaction between the woman and the care team. Arguably it is *this* interaction which makes the drug work and from which the evidence can be gathered, yet it goes unnoticed and is statistically insignificant, leaving only the correlation between drug prescription, administration and outcome. Returning to my original question, my contention is that in order to identify what is occurring between human beings that actually makes things work, we need to rethink the nature of what constitutes evidence. This can be done through a reflective process that I term *practice-based evidence.*

My main port of call in undertaking a discussion on practice-based evidence is the work of Della Fish (1998). Fish first develops a powerful critique of evidence-based practice as technical rationalism, following on from the work of Donald Schon. For Schon (1991: 42), the crucial issue is how professionals deal with the complexity of their working existence and, in parallel, with a doctrine of professional rules which serves a reductionist purpose to uphold their power base:

> In the varied topography of professional practice, there is a high, hard ground where practitioners can make effective use of research-based theory and technique, and there is a swampy lowland where situations are confusing 'messes' incapable of technical solution. The difficulty is that the problems of the high ground, however great their technical interest, are often unimportant to clients or to the larger society, while in the swamp are the problems of greatest human concern. Shall the practitioner stay on the high, hard ground where he can practice rigorously, as he understands rigor, but where he is constrained to

deal with problems of relatively little social importance? Or shall he descend to the swamp where he can engage the most important and challenging problems if he is willing to forsake technical rigor?

Fish (1998) builds on this notion and discusses how technical rationalism appears to have become the 'deity' in our modern lives, creating a framework by which we all live and within which we exist. Statistical evidence and the technology which creates it – the 'what works' agenda – are, she feels, the new gods to which homage is paid. For instance, Sackett *et al.*'s (1997) 'Hierarchy of Evidence' can be outlined as:

1   A: Systematic Reviews
    B: Randomised Control Trials
    C: Experimental Designs
2   A: Cohort Control Studies
    B: Case Control Studies
3   A: Consensus Conference
    B: Expert Opinion
    C: Observational Study
    D: Other Types of Study, e.g. Interview Based, Local Audit
    E: Quasi-Experimental; Qualitative Design
4   A: Personal Communication

In this model, qualitative design and personal communication – those qualities that form the basis of uncovering human experience for inquiry purposes – are the lowest in the hierarchy of what constitutes 'evidence'. It is that done *to* others which is considered powerful, not that done *with* them.

Fish (1998) suggests that we should become 'practitioner-researchers' in order to oppose this situation professionally. This is not done through the construction of some rigorous methodology whereby we go out and observe and tick some pre-ordained boxes; it is more akin to formulating questions based on observations of either our inner self or things we have witnessed. By this I mean the process of reflecting on experience, and the testing of these experiences within our own individual value bases and understanding. Coming back to those fundamental principles of evidence-based medicine in asking the right questions, being a practitioner-researcher can also be about asking the right questions, but in a way which is reflexive of the situation and the experience. We can question those we practise upon to discover more about their experience of their circum-stances, or about ourselves and our responses to the situations in which we find ourselves. But these questions are not diagnostic – they are ontological and empirical, for they are about furthering knowledge, in ways that deepen and uncover our knowledge of self and others.

However, no matter how laudable these principles are from a philosophical stance, they are problematic when seen from within the culture that exists in the current climate, for they are almost entirely subjective understandings. They have no concrete base to them, and are primarily individual perceptions – personal 'truths', for want of a better term, which cannot be generalised or counted, or that have no sound methodological basis from which they derive or create knowledge. They can be powerful, evocative, may move us psychologically, and may even involve critical thinking, but they are not scientific. And this is the cause of the tension.

As a demonstrator of how we can be moved and reflect through 'something other' than science, I want to try something out with you. I confess that I have blatantly borrowed some of Gary Rolfe's (2005) ideas. Below are two pieces of text to read; then some questions will be posed.

> I was still young enough then to be sleeping with my mother, which seemed to me life's whole purpose. We slept together in the first floor bedroom on a flock-filled mattress in a bed of brass rods and curtains. Alone, at that time, of all the family, I was her chosen dream companion, chosen from all for her extra love; my right, so it seemed to me.
>
> So in the ample night and the thickness of her hair I consumed my fattened sleep, drowsed and nuzzling to her warmth of flesh, blessed by her bed and safety. From the width of the house and the separation of the day, we two then lay joined alone.
>
> (Lee, 1962: 25)

> The sensitive, responsive behaviour of the caregiver in a secure dyad teaches the secure infant that communication is contingent upon each partner's cues and responses. The insensitive, uncoordinated interactions of an insecure dyad teach the insecure infant that communication is not a responsive interaction, but a series of poorly coordinated bids and responses. All infants carry forward not only the expectations of how interactions with social partners are coordinated, but also their experiences with caregivers in succeeding or failing to construct synchronous, reciprocal social and emotional exchanges.
>
> (Weinfield *et al.*, 2008: 85)

Now the questions:

- Which of these pieces creates a sense of memory of a time past?
- Which of these pieces do we engage with more fully as human beings?
- Which of these pieces enables us to engage with ourselves as unique individuals?

Both pieces have the concept of attachment theory at their core, but their approaches to its representation and experience are polarised. In theoretical terms there is no doubt that the second example would hold far more weight if put to the test scientifically, for it has been constructed as such through empirical testing. Yet Laurie Lee's narrative gives us something which the second piece cannot – a real sense of *being in* the moment – and as such we can find ourselves connecting to that experience, or of evoking a similar personal experience through which we are able to place ourselves in the experience that this narrative portrays.

The problem is that this type of internalisation and abstraction does not sit equally alongside technical rational practices with regard to its substance. It is more fully discussed in the area of research methodology and the debate between qualitative and quantitative approaches, where data collection approaches such as interviews and subsequent analysis methods which explore meaning and symbolism are not seen as equal to the supposed 'gold standard' research methodologies of double-blind randomised control trials (RCTs) because they cannot and deliberately do not eradicate the personal from the research process. This is an interesting notion, for it can be argued that the reductionist action of the RCTs has little or no intellectual quality to it, and that true intellectual engagement lies in the qualitative and reflective actions of 'softer' forms of research.

'Reflection': something about this word and the way it is used as a method of thinking has always puzzled me. What is a reflection? If, like me, what you see in the mirror in the morning is a *reflection of what is actually there* in front of it (not the most appealing of sights, I assure you) then surely a reflection is a representation of fact – or, at the very least, a mirror-image of it. Yet reflection as a learning tool or a way of thinking is considered without fact – a cognitive process fraught with ambiguity and subjectivity. True reflection, surely, would deal only in fact, representing what is fact, illuminating us with what is directly in front of us. So reflection is both the hardest and the most reductionist form of evidence we can have, is it not?

Well, yes . . . and no – depending on how you look at it. When we look back at an event 'reflectively', we change the emphasis on what we saw. The images are not clear to us – in fact, we do not see the whole image, only fragments of it, as Jean-Paul Sartre (1996) suggests, and our interpretations of them come from our own unique understandings and socialisation. These images do not come to us all as some kind of generalisable film show. Even two people watching the same event will interpret it differently and focus on different elements of it, so in this sense reflection is a fluffy ball of subjectivity. And yet the reflections we make, either at the time or after the event, are based on something empirical – our own knowledge foundation – our personal experiences, understandings and ways of being. They are matters which are there in our psyche. Attempts have even been made to break down and compartmentalise this process of thinking. The whole discipline of psychology has tried to form a scientific basis to its practice through measuring cognition, behaviour, etc., and creating propositions as to how these can be read and understood. Why? Because empirical clarity enables a power base to emerge that can be equivalent to that of medicine. It is born out of what is promoted as hard fact, and it is infinitely easier to manage this than what the term 'psychology' actually means – a science of the soul (*psyche* being Greek for 'soul'). The archetypal psychologist James Hillman (1992) argues that psychology has 'lost its soul' precisely for this reason. It is, he suggests, a dilution of what it means to be human if we are no longer interested in the working of the soul and what it tells us, only in how it can be viewed mechanically; and psychology is worse off as a result. Reflection leaves us with things that can be viewed both as real (for they are our own personal experiences which we live through when thinking of an event) and unreal (for precisely the same reasons, for they are not immediately evident and measurable, regarded only as a cognitive video that plays within our affective domain).

For the purposes of our immediate discussion, a definition of 'reflection' is necessary. Christopher Johns (2007: 3) provides a useful starting point: a general statement that reflection as a term is characterised as 'learning through experience toward new insights or changed perceptions of self and practice'. Within this, some core elements can be drawn out as contributing factors in its construction:

- Practical wisdom
- Reflexivity
- Becoming mindful
- Commitment
- Contradiction

- Understanding
- Empowerment

We will come back to these elements in Chapter 2, but we can already see how they are different to the way in which evidence-based practice is applied. How can concepts such as 'practical wisdom' and 'becoming mindful' be measured in concrete ways, or through some audit process? Moreover, can we really judge what is seen through our own eyes and thinking with that seen and thought by others as a measure of 'quality' in the way that an audit system demands? The answer, of course, is no, but that does not deny that these essences exist as opposites in how human behaviour can be interpreted and thought upon. It is these essences – those that are tied up in a complex knot of experience, interpretation, values, etc. which are so hard to place within a structure – that suffer as we strive to place them in the appropriate filing trays.

'Data without generalisation is just gossip' (Pirsig, 2006: 59). In *Lila*, Robert Pirsig tells of how factions of anthropologists in the late nineteenth century began to construct ways in which observations of culture could be broken down in the form of hard science, following rules generated through mathematics and physics in which no values should be attached in a mathematical sense to what is observed or found. All that remains, they argued, are objective facts, and these cannot be generalised, for the objective facts may not apply in other cultures. Similar approaches have been applied for many years by social scientists in a drive to be 'scientific'. But there is a problem with this, for in order to try to strengthen the science through reductionism, the context of the research becomes increasingly unique and impossible to generalise. In the end it becomes so unscientific that it is just 'gossip'. Reflection avoids this by admitting that it is not scientific in its approach. Johns' (2007) constituent elements of reflection, as we have noted, cannot be measured through control groups or statistical tests, but they are means through which a form of human inquiry can grow. What is different, perhaps, is that it is seen as lacking in rigour or structure, for it occurs haphazardly – chaotically even – with no set pattern. This, in the current climate, is problematic, for the 'what works' agenda does not see relevance in such nebulous matters, or in the way in which such knowledge comes about.

It is, however, the foundation of *practice-based evidenc* practice, whether they be in teaching, nursing, social w therapy, occur haphazardly. Few things in health and s society in general, are logical and consistent. It is probab the only consistency in life is its inconsistency. We const in new situations which in turn prompt new feelings, new challenges to our values, and new learning experiences. It is in these experiences that we make choices as practitioners: to sleepwalk through the experience and gain nothing new from it; or to engage with it in order to understand it and our self better through it.

Have you ever been driving your car and suddenly come to a point in the road where you are forced to ask yourself: how did I get here? You have watched the road, changed gear, applied the brakes, negotiated a roundabout, and suddenly you find yourself at a set of traffic lights unaware of how you got there because your mind has been elsewhere; a purely mechanical function has taken over and you have disengaged from its actions. This is what I mean by 'sleepwalking'. It is possible to sleepwalk through the working day. The hectic nature of much work in modern life even encourages it as a form of survival. In many ways, despite working in human services, the services themselves expect automaton-type function, for they are concerned with throughput and output, creating systematic human machinery models to achieve targets. Such an industrial model is an easy way to function. Machines do not need to think about what they are doing; they just do it. Reflection, conversely, is hard work. It involves confrontation of ourselves and our situations, and the problems we encounter when we do this.

Conclusion

A useful vignette for the kinds of conflict I describe above arises in *Star Trek Voyager*. In this, a member of the Borg – the ultimate in efficient species – Seven of Nine, is captured. Originally human, but now assimilated as Borg, the *Voyager* crew attempt to re-humanise her. As her genetic memory recovers and she is integrated into the crew, we see a struggle between being 'efficient' and a re-emergence of what it means to be human: to be flawed emotionally and physically. These human matters give her most conflict, for they are the hardest to acknowledge and confront. Ultimately, she remains a hybrid of the two, still efficient, yet able to rationalise the human psyche.

In a way, our human services have been going through a similar process. We have been assimilated. Resistance has been futile. However, reflection, either as a process of learning or as a method for engaging in research, gives us an opportunity to counter the effects of an audit- and evidence-obsessed culture, but only if we move away from the mechanistic application of models and approaches that currently characterises reflection amongst the health, education and social care professions. For this reason, as I wrote earlier, reflection is not working. If reflection can be reconstructed in workplace education and practice development as the intellectual, spiritual, creative and fulfilling activity that it really is, then we may regain some of what it really means to be human. 'Evidence' will still exist, but it will be of a different type.

Note

My potted history of medicine does the work of Brian Inglis and Roy Porter a great injustice. For anyone who has an interest in this field, I would recommend their texts. Despite its age, Inglis' work has a cohesive approach to its presentation, while Porter's is a fascinating and current account of medicine's history and its impact on economic, social and political life.

References

Bachelard, G. (1988) *Le Materialisme Rationnel*. In Canguilhem, G., *Ideology and Rationality in the History of the Life Sciences*. MIT Press. Cambridge, MA, and London

Beck, U. (1992) *Risk Society: Towards a New Modernity*. Sage. London

Canguilhem, G. (1988) *Ideology and Rationality in the History of the Life Sciences*. MIT Press. Cambridge, MA, and London

Cavailles, J. (1976) *Sur La Logique et la theorie de la science* (3rd edn). Vrin. Paris

Clarke, J. and Newman, J. (1997) *The Managerial State: Power, Politics, and Ideology in the Making of Social Welfare*. Sage. New York

Covell, D.G., Uman, G.C. and Manning, P.R. (1985) Information Needs in Office Practice: Are They Being Met? *Annals of Internal Medicine*. 103(4): 596–9

Dawes, M. (2005) Evidence-Based Practice. In Dawes, M., Davies, P., Gray, A., Mant, J., Seers, K. and Snowball, R., *Evidence-Based Practice: A Primer for Health Care Professionals*. Elsevier. London

Dawes, M., Davies, P., Gray, A., Mant, J., Seers, K. and Snowball, R. (2005) *Evidence-Based Practice: A Primer for Health Care Professionals*. Elsevier. London

Dawes, M. and Uchechukwu, S. (2003) Knowledge and Management in Clinical Practice: A Systematic Review of Information-Seeking Behaviour in Physicians. *International Journal of Medical Informatics*. 70(1): 9–15

Emmison, M. and Smith, P. (2002) *Researching the Visual*. Sage. London

Fish, D. (1998) *Appreciating Practice in the Caring Professions*. Blackwell Science. Oxford

Freshwater, D. and Rolfe, G. (2004) *Deconstructing Evidence-Based Practice*. Routledge. London and New York

Giddens, A. (1991) *The Consequences of Modernity*. Polity. Cambridge

Hillman, J. (1992) *Re-visioning Psychology*. Harper Perennial. London

Illich, I. (1977) *Disabling Professions*. Marion Boyars. London

Inglis, B. (1965) *A History of Medicine*. Weidenfeld and Nicolson. London

Johns, C. (2007) *Becoming a Reflective Practitioner*. Blackwell. Oxford

Lee, L. (1962) *Cider with Rosie*. Penguin. London

McSherry, R., Simmons, M. and Pearce, P. (2002) An Introduction to Evidence-Informed Nursing. In McSherry, R., Simmons, M. and Abbott, P., *Evidence-Informed Nursing: A Guide for Clinical Nurses*. Routledge. London and New York

McWhinney, I.R. (1995) Why We Need a New Clinical Method. In Stewart, M., Belle Brown, J., Weston, W., McWhinney, I.R., McWilliam, C.L and Freeman, T.R., *Patient-Centred Medicine: Transforming the Clinical Method*. Sage. London

Pirsig, R. (2006) *Lila: An Inquiry into Morals*. Alma Books. Richmond

Porter, R. (1996) *Cambridge Illustrated History: Medicine*. Cambridge University Press. Cambridge

Power, M. (1997) *The Audit Society: Rituals of Verification*. Oxford University Press. Oxford

Ramachandran, V.S. (2005) *Phantoms in the Brain*. Harper Perennial. London

Rolfe, G. (2000) *Research, Truth, Authority: Postmodern Perspectives on Nursing*. Macmillan Press. London

Rolfe, G. (2005) Keynote Presentation: International Mixed Methods in Health and Social Care Conference. The Moller Centre, Cambridge, UK, 11–12 July

Sackett, D.L., Strauss, S.E., Scott Richardson, W., Rosenberg, W. and Brian Haynes, R. (1997/2000) *Evidence-based Medicine: How to Practice and Teach EBM*. Churchill Livingstone. London

Sartre, J.P. (1996) *Being and Nothingness*. Routledge. London

Schon, D. (1991) *The Reflective Practitioner: How Professionals Think in Action*. Arena. Aldershot

Trinder, L. (2001) The Context of Evidence-based Practice. In Trinder, L. and Reynolds, S., *Evidence-based Practice: A Critical Appraisal*. Blackwell Science. Oxford

Weinfield, N.S., Sroufe, L.A., Egeland, B. and Carlson, E. (2008) Individual Differences in Infant-Caregiver Attachment: Conceptual and Empirical Aspects of Security. In Cassidy, J. and Shaver, P.R., *Handbook of Attachment: Theory, Research, and Clinical Applications*. The Guilford Press. New York and London

Yalom, I.D. (2005) *When Nietzsche Wept*. Harper Perennial. New York

Chapter 2

The relationship between reflection and action research

It is a mistake to believe that the decisive moments of a life when its direction changes for ever must be marked by sentimental loud and shrill dramatics, manifested by violent inner surges. This is a sentimental fairy tale invented by drunken journalists, flashbulb happy film-makers and readers of the tabloids. In truth, the dramatic moments of a life-determining experience are often unbelievably low-key. It has so little in common with the bang, the flash, or the volcanic eruption that, at the moment it happens, the experience is often not even noticed. When it unfolds its revolutionary effect, and ensures that life is revealed in a brand-new light, with a brand-new melody, it does that silently and in this wonderful silence resides its special nobility.

(Mercier, 2009: 38)

Introduction

The aim of this chapter is to examine the nature of reflection and action research, identifying where similar properties exist between the two, and where there are distinct differences. I wish to explore ways in which these two ways of thinking and uncovering can be conceptualised and structured, for both have a foundation which is essentially grounded in ways of being – in a sense phenomenological, but which can be applied in practical ways to enhance function and understanding, either of an organisation or of the self. It has to be recognised that practical ways of engaging in these methods cannot be achieved without the ability to think reflectively, so, for instance, whilst a model to conduct an action research study can be constructed systematically and a reflective model can be used to aid thinking, neither can be effective unless those who engage in it are comfortable with whatever the reflective process may bring. In this sense one cannot ignore the ethical issues that may arise in such work or the realisation that the undertaking of 'action' is far more complex than first considered. In addition, I will discuss some of the more traditional matters that have guided researchers in the fields of anthropology, ethnography and phenomenology with regard to how the 'researcher' in the field manages the issues of self in the research process. These are matters that can only be managed reflexively. In that sense the similarities and differences between the terms 'reflection' and 'reflexivity' are explored. Following this is the observation that many books on 'reflective practice' discuss this in abstract from its philosophical roots. In my experience of working with professional groups who are expected to reflect, the fundamental skills of learning how to reflect are generally overlooked in designing curricula, leading, in the main, to descriptive and non-reflective accounts of practice and experiences of learning. I have therefore included a section within this chapter that focuses specifically on philosophical thinking around reflection.

In no way do I intend to do expansive justice to the vast amount of literature available in these fields. My aim is merely to provide a flavour of their use.

Action research

Greenwood and Levin (1998) provide a useful account of the origins of action research stemming from the work of Kurt Lewin and the scientific outlining of General Systems Theory (GST). In a scientific sense, GST refers to the way in which the world is organised – atoms, molecules and interactive systems which form in different ways to create the vast array of experiences that we encounter in the world. Lewin's work as applied to social sciences, beginning in the 1940s, formed the basis for experimentation in natural settings with a profound impact on social change through planned and systematic approaches to participation in the change process. Greenwood and Levin's argument is that through these embryonic roots action research has the potential to be the most scientific form of qualitative research, and that it is wrong-headed to see action research as non-scientific. GST is transposed in action research from a theory of physics or biology to one of participation and action, but it is through GST that action research is given its scientific rigour.

Morton-Cooper (2000) suggests that action research may not be a method of research at all, or even a set of methods, but a way of approaching the study of human beings from a philosophical construct in which some form of sharing takes place within mutually supportive environments. It is therefore, in this view, a *critically reflexive* approach to research in which claims of validity to knowledge within a particular domain can be examined and contested, which in this process help to generate new ways of thinking, seeing and acting. Following on from Chapter 1 and its discussion of the practitioner-researcher and the constitution of evidence, it is useful to put this approach in context.

Action research as an approach to human inquiry has emerged from, and exists as an approach whilst living within, a culture that is heavily weighted towards a technical or positivist paradigm with regard to practice and governance. And, as has previously been outlined, stability (albeit superficial) is felt to have been created through this paradigm (Weil, 1999). As a discipline of inquiry, action research therefore has the potential to destabilise this position because one of its guiding principles is that it is democratic. It aims to close the gap between the researcher and the researched upon, therefore negating positions of power in the research process itself, but in so doing it can be perceived as being subversive as opposed to democratic. Morton-Cooper (2000) goes on to suggest that within the current prevailing political and scientific paradigm, the deregulation of services and economies seen throughout health and social care systems has led to a tendency towards increased state control and intervention – and this can be seen through the application of evidence-based practice, clinical governance, competency based education, and increased regulation under the guise of 'quality'. This is an interesting notion in itself, as it is felt that 'quality' can somehow be measured; but what is quality to one may not be quality to another. In Robert Pirsig's *Zen and the Art of Motorcycle Maintenance* and the follow-up *Lila* (cited in Chapter 1), the main character Phaedrus is consumed by trying to establish a *Metaphysics of Quality*, which ultimately means traversing around an ever-deepening circle of inquiry. The nature of action research is that it is designed to explore concepts of quality and value, but that they are uncovered democratically in the exploration, not imposed as pre-ordained constructs. John Elliott (1991: 51) locates this notion within the construct of values in relation to practice, the reflective process, and where action research sits within it:

> When values define the ends of a practice, such ends should not be viewed as concrete objectives or targets which can be perfectly raised at some future point in time. As such they would constitute technical ends which can be clearly specified in advance of practice. Inasmuch as reflection is involved, it constitutes technical reasoning about how to bring about a prespecified end-product. Values as ends cannot be

clearly defined independently of and prior to practice. In this context the practice itself constitutes an interpretation of its ends in a particular practical situation. The ends are defined in practice and not in advance of it.

What Elliott suggests here is that there is a possibility of a technical rational approach to reflection – that as long as what is reflected upon enables the meeting of the necessary end then reflection has served its purpose. There are some very real examples of this in education and practice through using reflective models, such as Kolb and Gibbs', for example, which have been reduced to quite positivistic use in order to evidence the learner's or practitioner's 'reflection'. But, of course, it can be so much more, as Elliott (1991: 51) goes on to say:

> The kind of reflection involved here is quite different to technical means-end reasoning. It is both ethical and philosophical. Inasmuch as the reflection is about choosing a course of action in a particular set of circumstances, to realize one's own values, it is ethical in character. But since ethical choice implies an interpretation of the values to be realized, reflection about means cannot be separated from reflection about ends. Ethical reflection has a philosophical dimension.

The nature of action research, for Elliott, is reflective. Indeed, what Schon and others term 'reflective practice', he terms 'action research'. For Elliott, action research is fundamentally about the transformation of practice. Its role is not purely philosophical, though he recognises that it has philosophical qualities. It is an empirical approach to the importance of data in reflectively improving practice. It is not merely the application of reflection to practice to achieve an aim or end-product – such as the way in which reflection is used to validate a professional value base in learners, for instance in nursing or social work – but the quality of the data that is collected to achieve it. Reflection and the quality of data are therefore intertwined, for in Elliott's view one cannot improve upon the methodology of action research without considering philosophical reflection. In this sense action research can take forms which are 'clinical' (such as Schein, 2008) or socio-technical (such as Passmore, 2008) as examples if they are inclusive of critical reflection.

Richard Winter (1989) discusses the problems of action research and positivism by looking at the nature of professional knowledge, and in particular at what is an authoritative body of knowledge in some forms of professional work, but continuously open to question in others – so 'getting it right in advance' (such as in planning and execution) in professions such as teaching, nursing and social work is more tenuous than 'getting it right in advance' in an engineering sense. Winter suggests that teachers can never be sure that a curriculum is going to work in the way that an engineer might expect a bridge to work, for, as with nursing, social work and other human interaction work, the exercising of their expertise can never be an exercising of general rules and will always require some self-conscious analysis. Somekh (2006) cites the work of Schostak (1999: 401), who suggests that 'competent action is simply not possible for anyone' because it is impossible to project all eventualities to actions, and as such an action cannot have an entirely rational outcome or a complete grasp of the issue. In practice, suggests Somekh, this is the position of action research. The collection and analysis of data creates a stronger basis for the taking of action, but the grasp of whatever is at hand is necessarily always incomplete rather than fully apprehended.

Out of this notion comes the need for a research methodology that can take account of changing situations from the 'inside' which is not reliant upon positivist assumptions, but which is also able to defend itself in the face of accusations of bias, or of relying on anecdotal evidence. Winter (1989), like Elliott (1991), supports the view that this form of research is located firmly within the realm of the practitioner, and as such provides an interpretation of the way in which this process takes place. He identifies three 'scales':

- *1 Small scale*: this describes the kinds of informed and thoughtful decision-making that routinely characterise professional work.
- *2 The largest scale*, whereby the outcomes of administrative decisions are monitored. These have most relevance to management processes.
- *3 The in-between scale*, which is where Winter sees the problems of action research arising. He suggests that action research falls between scales 1 and 2 and should be more elaborate than scale 1 and less elaborate than scale 2, because the purpose of action research is not merely to identify and maintain patterns, but to change them, and such research is likely to be of small samples, which are therefore not sufficiently representative to claim validity.

This fits with Elliott's (1991) expression of *means–end reasoning*, leading to a conclusion that this form of research has a different form of ethical nature to that of trying to provide generalisability. However, given that action research exists as a field of inquiry alongside an overarching positivist approach to knowledge, a culture of managerialism and fetish with the use of audits, Winter (1989: 37) provides us with a number of questions whose answers may deem it a more mainstream methodology:

- How can action research be economical?
- How can action research procedures be specific?
- How can action research procedures be accessible?
- How can action research procedures be rigorous?

Because these questions are aimed at a research methodology which is grounded in the ethics of reflection, the same questions can be aimed at the reflective process, too. There is, of course, a further question to this thinking: whether it is right that both of these approaches to knowledge should be forced to conform in some reductionist way to a mode of thought constrained by limits to practice and function. For, as Jean MacNiff (2003: 5) writes, 'I have become certain of the need for uncertainty.'

Action research can be seen from different viewpoints in terms of its use. For instance, there is 'educational action research', 'participatory action research' and 'action science'. Whilst there are some discreet differences in how these approaches are conceptualised, there are also some underpinning principles. Like Morton-Cooper (2000), MacNiff (2003) feels that, in one way, this 'action research' thing does not exist. She suggests it is not some self-contained inquiry process that exists separately from us – a set of procedures which are applied to practice through some abstract approach. It is fundamental that discussions about action research should be inclusive of real-life experiences of real-life people, for the 'meaning' of action research is found within the way in which people live alongside one another. The question of whether action research exists does not lead MacNiff to claim that there are no action researchers, but it raises further questions as to what action researchers do, how and why they do it, how they view themselves, how they come to know, and what they hope to achieve. These interrelated questions are not of researcher activity and behaviour, but of researcher values and actions. On conducting action research, MacNiff begins to tease out some positions that researchers may take on their activities. She suggests that they are constantly critiquing their practice so that learning from this can progress to purposeful personal action for social benefit. In this, action research is concerned with ideas of social justice, compassionate ways of living, respect for diversity and ideas of truth. She suggests that action researchers, and therefore action research itself, often live in contexts where the values outlined above are esteemed in principle, but denied in reality – the reality being that preference is shown to privileged elites rather than to those who are marginalised or underprivileged. Action researchers, and therefore action research itself, aim to explore and understand these issues so that there may be changes that reflect the values above.

Action researchers, from MacNiff's (2003) perspective, see knowledge as what they do. It is never complete and it is constantly shifting and developing as new and different understandings emerge. It becomes a way of being that is full of potential, surprises and unpredictability, so absolute answers to questions become meaningless, because whatever is found becomes a new question. Learning is therefore rooted firmly in experience: the experiences are reflected upon in the light of the researcher's values and then future actions can be decided upon. Whilst techniques such as critical incident analysis can be used to construct this kind of learning in formal ways, it can also be enacted through a process of critical awareness – being active in practice as a form of intellectual study rather than my earlier description of 'sleepwalking' through it.

In relation to the way in which action researchers act, MacNiff (2003) sees a central role in enabling choices of identity and collaboration to take place through appreciating another's point of view. This is not necessarily to create harmony or consensus, but more importantly to create an environment for negotiating differences and tolerance. The reflection on the action element of the process, inherent in action research methodology, supports this form of researcher activity when it is applied dialogically through the reflective encounter. MacNiff sees the ideas of encounter, connectedness and relationship as a form of spirituality when applied to herself. When I apply it to *myself* I see it as a form of transcendence. The idea of connectedness suggests that we are always in relation with someone, and that relationship has the potential to change lives, so action research is consequently tied up amongst such relationships. Action research is, in my view, transcendent.

In one sense, then, action research is grounded in an eclectic mixture of philosophical thinking around transcendence, of ethical thinking around values, and of recognition that it operates in a domain of uncertainty as to how it apprehends the nature of an 'action'. But this is insufficient to place it – even as an ideology – within a field of inquiry. Somekh (2006) lays down a series of methodological principles for action research which take us from an important but nebulous stage of thinking to something more concrete, which has practical application. For her (Somekh, 2006: 6–8), a definition of action research is based around eight key components:

- Action research integrates research and action.
- Action research is conducted by a collaborative partnership of participants and researchers.
- Action research involves the development of knowledge and understanding of a unique kind.
- Action research starts from a vision of social transformation and aspirations for greater social justice for all.
- Action research involves a high level of reflexivity.
- Action research involves exploratory engagement with a wide range of existing knowledge.
- Action research engenders powerful learning for participants.
- Action research locates the inquiry in an understanding of broader historical, political and ideological contexts.

Broadly speaking, Somekh constructs action research as a series of holistic and flexible cycles: the collection, analysis and interpretation of data interwoven with planning and introduction of action strategies which are evaluated through the same process, and so on, until the intensity of the inquiry reduces. In this sense it is ongoing, even if the 'project' reaches a conclusion. Partnerships formed from those working both inside and outside of the field of study contribute to it equally, or differentiating members of the field of inquiry come together with an aspiration to establish an environment of equality and esteem in the way in which the data is gathered and interpreted. Change and development are perceived as natural occurrences rather than constructed, and the work engaged in is not seen as value neutral, such as is aspired to in scientific research; it is the opposite, with aims to promote social justice through politically informed stances and personal engagement, enabling access to mechanisms of power through which influence and direction to change can occur. Further, it fundamentally sees the researcher as intermeshed amongst personal and professional relationships through which a researcher identity emerges which empowers a sense of capacity to improve working practices, relationships and outcomes of the action research itself. In order to achieve this, existing theoretical knowledge is drawn from a wide range of sources and disciplines, such as philosophy, psychology and sociology. This knowledge can be tested as to its usefulness, exploring the suitable application of ideas to the field of study and where necessary building on theories in ways which refine and illuminate the data. Then there is the reflective process itself, and the capacity for the researcher to understand in what ways personal values and assumptions have moulded the research findings and the subsequent questions as to the quality of the research. Finally, there is the political element to the research: the ideology and economic factors which constrain human activities, and the way in which 'insiders' and 'outsiders', or other collaborators, come to see different realities and perspectives through engaging interprofessionally and interpersonally in the action research process.

Ideas that support reflection

A number of thinkers and writers have begun to construct how reflection can be structured, and I turn to them now.

It is reasonable to assume that reflection as a process is rooted in an interpretivist paradigm. By this I mean that it is concerned with approaches that share a set of subjectivist assumptions around the nature of social order and lived experiences. My starting point for this lies within continental philosophy, starting with the German philosophical phenomenologists Hegel and Husserl, and then the French thinkers Jean-Paul Sartre and Maurice Merleau-Ponty. We should also look at the work of the American social phenomenologist Alfred Schutz.

Taken chronologically, Friedrich Hegel is the earliest of the thinkers in this area. Changeux and Ricoeur (2000), in a discussion of Hegel's *Phenomenology of Mind*, find that the intention of phenomenology is to examine the *sensible history* of the mind. In this work there is a belief that there is not a presumed end or horizon of meaning – in other words, what we live through and observe will not lead us to the same conclusion as others, for it is a matter of personal interpretation based on what we already believe we know. Hegel presents his understanding of life experiences as progressive, moving through a series of thresholds of thought, in the process of which there are increases of meaning. He claims there is more meaning in perception than in sensation, more in the concept than in perception, more in theoretical reasoning than in the concept, and increasingly so on until there is more in a communal experience than in an individual consciousness. Here he is saying that we progress from feeling something to perceiving what it may be; from that, we conceive what is occurring and it becomes rationalised through a complexity of what is known and understood personally. At some point it is made available to others through expression and enters a different type of consciousness – something more collective and shared. For Changeux and Ricoeur, Hegel is important because of this understanding of the graduated process through which an augmentation of meaning occurs, which in turn prompts evaluation and complexity of thinking. Hegel uses the term 'sensible history' to denote this process, which could be reformed for the purposes of reflection as a 'history of individual sensibility'. Hegel's work is complex and dense, and he grapples with properties that he feels exist between unique individuals and collective individuals – for him, there is a certain type of 'I' which is unique, and another which is generalisable (see Hegel, 1991). These properties can be experienced both internally and externally, for there are ways in which we conceive ('picture thinking', as he describes it) which are unique or singular, and ways in which we express – for instance, through language and forms of behaviour – where we find there are others who have experienced similarly, and as such these matters are generalisable.

The work of Edmund Husserl appears to take us on a different type of diversion. For Husserl, phenomenology is an attempt to describe our experiences directly, as they are, and separately from their origins and development. He suggests that it is not the case that one thing follows on from another, so we should not imagine that they do as a natural progression. This forms part of his wider refutation that as science grows and develops its findings, things *must be* the case. The first meditation within his book *Cartesian Meditations* (1967) is devoted partly to the subject of science and a guarding against the *matter of course* opinion of science. He focuses on what he terms *transcendental subjectivity* as a way to develop his refutation:

> [W]e now have neither a science that we accept nor a world that exists for us. Instead of simply existing for us – that is being accepted naturally by us in our experiential believing in its existence – the world is for us something that claims being . . . In short, not just corporeal Nature but the whole concrete surrounding life-world is for me, from now on, only a phenomenon of being instead of something that is.
>
> (Husserl, 1967: 18–19)

Here, Husserl is trying to say that the work of science has led us from a feeling of being part of the world into an exploration of how we function within it – a kind of cause-and-effect mentality to our existence in a world that happens around us. He further suggests that although this appears to be the case, we do not wish to accept the science that has constructed it. In opposition to this, Husserl argues the case for transcendental subjectivity, and explores the consideration that for each kind of actual experience, which we assume to be universal in our consciousness through our common understandings of them, such as perception, retention, recollection and so on, there is a corresponding 'as-if' experience with its own parallel fields (as-if perception, as-if retention, as-if recollection and so on). Through these parallel fields we make judgements as to the way in which rules of first-hand actualities and first-hand possibilities are understood. In the simplest terms, the transcendent subjectivity is in the 'as-if' expression of an actual event, where the speaker talks of it as an 'as-if' event – 'It was as-if he was in the room.' We are not talking of the actuality; we are talking of its possibility. This is the transcendence – we can place abstraction into actuality and it begins to make sense for the listener. This, in itself, is a reflective property: it is reciprocally understood by all parties involved and has universality very different to that of the scientific paradigm.

Alfred Schutz's work in social phenomenology follows on from Husserl's to a degree, for it utilises the notion of transcendent subjectivity, but applies it in much more practical ways, differing in his use of previous experiences as contributory factors to reality. He sees social phenomenology as being about the ways people in society constitute and reconstitute everyday life. In effect, this examines the way in which the taken-for-granted world is produced and experienced by those living in it. Schutz (1964) feels that this approach safeguards the subjectivity of the social reality for those living through it, protecting it from what he describes as a fictional, non-existent world constructed by scientific observers.

Schutz (1970) also examines the notion of commonsense knowledge and the types of practical reasoning that individuals use to 'objectify' social forms. Holstein and Gubrium (1994) find that in his work, humans approach their lifeworld through a stock of knowledge made up of socially originated constructs and categories made up of images, theories, ideas, values and attitudes. These are then applied to experiences, which in turn become meaningful. 'Meaning requires the interpretive application of a category to the concrete particulars of a situation' (Holstein and Gubrium, 1994: 263). However, it is important to recognise these stocks of knowledge as open-ended constructs, constantly open to modification and adaptation, for the stock of knowledge grows as experiences take place. A further argument in Schutz's approach is the transformation from experience to language, and therefore, by default, meaning. In this view, consciousness typifies – it places the experience in a category – and language is the central medium for the transmission of these typologies and, subsequently, meaning itself. Language is used to convey meaning and describe reality. Social life and social phenomenology are located within a field of relationships between language use and objects of experience, and at its basis lies the belief that social interactions construct, as well as convey, meaning.

Jean-Paul Sartre, in his seminal *Being and Nothingness* (1996), discusses the problem of the connection between consciousness, immediate time, lapses of time and reflection. A fundamental question to his thinking on this is how reflection is possible for a sense of being which can be only in the past. Using the writing of Husserl and Descartes, who present reflection as an apprehension of consciousness immediately available to us, he asks whether a sense of being can exist from a time past, or whether all we will ever be is how we are at the most immanent moment of the reflection. Reflection, he suggests, is a new consciousness, and we live symbiotically with the new consciousness and the one reflected upon. He suggests that reflection is a witness to a consciousness, but rather than the witness (the reflection) providing an accurate account of that consciousness (that which is reflected upon), the reflected upon is altered profoundly by the reflection because it is self-conscious. In other words, our consciousness knows it is being observed by the reflection, so although both types of being exist as two parts of a separate consciousness, one feels it is being watched by an 'outside' observer, much like a student undergoing a direct observation of their practice. As a result, it plays itself out in a particular role – not necessarily a re-enactment but more an enactment of how it wishes to be seen. For Sartre, a consciousness which is reflected upon undergoes a profound modification of its being: it is no longer what it was at the moment when it was apprehended.

Sartre (1996) extends this discussion on reflection by dividing it into two kinds: pure reflection, the ideal and original form of reflection; and impure or accessory reflection. Reflection, he presupposes, is knowledge. It is characterised by a positional view and affirms the consciousness reflected upon. But there are certain conditions to this, for it can also work to negate and deny the 'I' of the object. 'To know', as Sartre (1996: 155) puts it, 'is to make oneself other.' The reflection itself and that reflected upon cannot wholly separate and as such cannot be grasped from a 'point of view'; rather, a sudden flood of knowledge arrives from no central point of departure and without a journey end-point.

> [T]he reflection which delivers the reflected-on to us, not as a given but as the being which we have to be, in indistinction without a point of view, is a knowledge overflowing itself and without explanation. At the same time it is never surprised by itself; it does not teach us anything but only posits.
>
> (Sartre, 1996: 155)

It is therefore paradoxical that reflection can be thought of as an authentic knowledge only if it is accepted that every reflection is, in fact, inauthentic. The motivation of reflection therefore serves two simultaneous purposes: to objectify and to interiorise through a unified process, enabling us to see things in a way in which we believe we understand them, and as a range of possibilities.

Maurice Merleau-Ponty (2003) discusses this from a slightly different perspective. His thoughts are centrally those of sense experience – or more accurately that we are aware of our existence through sensory experience. On discussing the sensory experience of spatial awareness, touch and the tactile perception of space, Merleau-Ponty suggests that there is no such way of drawing facts from the experience of being within a space; and, if it were possible, the 'facts' would require interpretation, leading to a conclusion of 'facts'. This problem, he suggests, 'belongs to the domain of reflection and not that of the experiment as the empiricist understands it, which is also as scientists understand it when they dream of an absolute objectivity' (Merleau-Ponty, 2003: 253).

Merleau-Ponty (2003) goes on to discuss two forms of reflection, the first of which is intellectualist reflection, which thematises the reflective object and the way in which consciousness is employed to lead the reflection to a concrete concept where it becomes 'what it is' – fixed and unchangeable. This form of consciousness, suggests Merleau-Ponty, has no sense of itself. It exists in a mechanical form and its understanding is universal, and the reflective object or experience exists only on the condition that it is central and unique to the 'I' that conceived it. The second form is radical reflection. For Merleau-Ponty (2003: 254), this is 'what takes hold of me as I am in the act of forming and formulating the ideas of subject and object, and brings to light the source of these two ideas; it is reflection, not only in operation, but conscious of itself in operation'. In other words, it is being conscious of a consciousness in operation as it conceives the reflection. This understanding of analytical reflection is one whereby the subject or object is not merely grasped as an idea, as intellectualist reflection would, but in which the reflection itself is an experience. This is fundamental to the difference between using reflective models in a mechanistic sense, and experiencing the act of reflection itself. As Merleau-Ponty (2003: 254) continues: 'by reflecting I put myself back inside that subject without finite limits, that I was before, and put back the object among the relations which previously subtended to it'. In effect, Merleau-Ponty confirms the thinking of Sartre (1996), but presents it differently and more clearly. He suggests that there are two forms of consciousness: one which is happy to play around with a reflection until it is satisfied that it is the 'right' conclusion, which becomes permanent; and a second which observes from the sidelines and has the capacity to take the reflection and place it in a field of possibility. But, like other human skills, it needs to be revealed and practised in order to become a skill.

More recent thinking on reflection and professional practice

Reflection as a skill? Is reflection something that can be learned in some technical way, as a clinical procedure or an interpersonal interaction may be learned? It is hard to categorise reflection in the same way as these examples, but there are some similarities in how we come to understand how to do these things which are primarily to do with our knowledge of them and the way in which we are guided to practise them. It has for some time been an expectation for learners and indeed researchers in the qualitative domain to reflect upon the experience of learning and researching and what is found through these experiences. And yet often people are not prepared or equipped for these activities; they are merely advised or required to do it and to provide evidence that they have done it. It is through this expectation that models of reflection have come to be significant in the learning lives of those in health and social care and education. But, arguably, if the foundations of the purposes of reflection, its aims and how it can become accessible to aid learning are not present, then the reflections evidenced are superficial; there for the purposes of assessment and nothing more. As a matter of contention, I argue that reflective practice as it is taught and practised now is failing for these reasons. Reflecting becomes real and works when it is understood, not when it is required as an outcome.

The seminal work of Donald Schon (1983) began to analyse the way in which professionals think in action. Primarily, he saw a model of preparation for professional life as one which supplied technical knowledge relevant to the practice of that discipline, but which failed to provide the capacity to work through complexity associated with any professional activity. It is through Schon's work that the terms of thinking *in action* (i.e. while doing something) and *on action* (i.e. after it has been done) have come to have significance in recent professional education. Schon's argument is that whilst professionals are able to deal with the specifics of their discipline, they are ill equipped to manage the human interactional relationships between that discipline and its impact on social life.

Schon (1983) uses a range of professional activities to describe this, including architecture, town planning and psychotherapy – all grounded in specific knowledge as enclosed disciplines, but when released into the real world of population consultation, such as in town planning, becoming highly charged, with unforeseen layers of complexity to be managed and worked through.

As a result, the concept of critical reflection in adult learning began to permeate into professional education through the work of people such as Jack Mezirow. Mezirow (1990: 14) focused particularly on 'transformative learning', suggesting that:

> Perspective transformation is the process of becoming critically aware of how and why our pre-suppositions have come to constrain the way we perceive, understand, and feel about our world; of re-formulating these assumptions to permit a more inclusive, discriminative, permeable, and integrative perspective; and of making decisions or otherwise acting on these new understandings. More inclusive, discriminating, permeable and integrative perspectives that adults choose if they can because they are motivated to better understand the meaning of their experience.

As with Schon's notions of how professionals think, presuppositions based on technical professional knowledge assume that things will just happen as planned because the knowledge suggests it. But, of course, this is not the case. It then becomes important, as Mezirow (1990) indicates, to enter into an act of transformation whereby what we believe we know becomes reformulated as understanding the meaning of an experience which has emerged not as a technical rational puzzle to be solved in the 'high ground' of professional knowledge but in the 'swampy lowlands' of human interaction (Schon, 1983). This has led to a variety of models and principles collectively known as 'reflective practice', which are practised within professional education and practice.

Ghaye and Ghaye (1998: 16–18) suggest ten principles of reflective practice, which I have precised below:

1 It needs to be understood as a set of meanings, statements, stories, etc., which produce a particular version of events. This reflective discourse – or conversation – is at the heart of the improvement process.
2 It is fuelled and energised by experience. Reflecting on something is our experience and all that it comprises. Reflecting on experience

is a way of interrogating our actions and thinking in particular ways.

3 It means returning to re-look at our taken-for-granted values, professional understanding and practices. It is not about reflecting on the extraordinary; it is about the ordinary, everyday occurrences of the working day. In this 'reflective turn' we consider the parts played by ourselves and others in these occurrences so that we may deepen our understanding of them.

4 It is about learning to explain and justify the way we go about things.

5 It means considering what we do 'problematically' – by constantly inquiring and questioning what we do systematically so that we may learn continuously from it.

6 It means putting what we know and learn to use, and informing improvement – by doing something positive and constructive through the knowledge we create which is purposeful. Engaging in thinking around what interests will be served through this process is important.

7 It means applying critical thinking to practice by asking probing or challenging questions, both of self and collectively so that transformation can take place.

8 It is a way of decoding the symbolic landscape around us – for example, why an environment is equipped in the way that it is, the way in which human relations occur, what appears significant or worthy within the environment, and the way in which these things are responded to. Symbolism is an important element in the reflective discourse.

9 It is a linkage between theoretical knowledge and practical application, enabling practitioners to create meaningful theories of action that are live and real.

10 It is eclectic, and is comfortable with drawing on different ways of knowing. It is not prejudiced in how knowledge is gained or understood and acts as an intersection between different approaches.

Having an appreciation of these principles and implementing them are, of course, two different things, for in order to act upon them there needs to be some guidance. One way of developing knowledge of reflective principles into the skill of reflection is through a 'reflective conversation' (Ghaye and Ghaye, 1998). Although the Ghayes refer specifically to teaching in this discussion, there is easy transfer into other disciplines, so I refer to 'the practitioner' in more general terms, replacing the Ghayes' 'the teacher'.

Broadly, Ghaye and Ghaye (1998) outline the reflective conversation as one which considers and questions the values that the practitioner is committed to – the values that give shape, form and purpose to professional practice. These conversations may initially be private conversations with the 'self', but at some point they are articulated with others. In doing so forms of language are tested in relation to description, justification, explanation and, where needed, persuasion, confrontation and encouragement. Moving from thoughts to words can sometimes be difficult, for attaching words to thoughts and feelings can be troublesome and uncomfortable. Finding the right word can be a challenge. However, moving from the private to public through this process can be enlightening, for it emerges out of unconscious into conscious forms of knowing (Polanyi, 1958, cited in Ghaye and Ghaye, 1998). It is through finding the right words that an understanding occurs. There are, of course, issues as to what remains confidential or hidden within the private and public conversations and that which is opened to the public domain more broadly, ultimately based on what is in the best interests of the practitioner, the organisation or the service user.

The reflective conversation is often one of questions and responses. These may be internal or external, but asking the right questions – similar to the way in which physicians ask questions in order to make a diagnosis – is fundamental to creating the dialogue. Questions such as 'What is my practice like? Why is it like this? How has it come to be this way? What are the effects of my practice on service users? How can I improve what I do?' enable a critical distance to practice and the context in which it takes place – a kind of differential diagnosis from which, in this case, new knowledge rather than a form of treatment can occur. It is also important that the questions look not only backwards but forwards. Exploration and justification of previous practice should not be the only preoccupations: there should also be some consideration of future possibilities and of what may develop.

The contexts of these types of conversation can obviously vary. They may be between pupil and teacher, mentor or practice teacher and student, clinical supervisor and practitioner, research student and supervisor, or any other combination, but generally one will be the owner of the experience upon which they are reflecting, while the other acts as the 'dialogical other', performing as helper, challenger and facilitator. Their role should be one of balance – exploring real and perceived weakness with structure and support in identifying and articulating strengths.

As Ghaye and Ghaye (1998) go on to note, enlightenment and empowerment are at the heart of such conversations through making sense of what is experienced and practised. In this sense, the reflective conversation can be applied in different ways, depending on the needs of the 'owner' of the reflection and which stage of reflection they are at. For students, a structure which introduces them to the practice of reflection in a more rigorous form through supervision may be of most use – as, for instance, in social work education – whilst for experienced practitioners a conversation where wisdom is more equally shared can be of benefit as both explore experiences and understandings through which a more synergistic knowledge can arise.

Reflective conversation is, however, not the only type of conversation. Reflective conversations are by their nature dialogic as opposed to, for instance, a debate where one person hopes to be victorious over another by overpowering their point of view. Johns (2004) sees this difference as non-collaborative and collaborative forms of communication. The non-collaborative forms, such as debate, reflect rivalry and power relationships, with the aim of winning the argument. A partial listening takes place, but only to tune into the parts of the conversation which will enable a reinforcing of the hearer's position, rather than opening up any wider possibilities of discussion. A collaborative dialogue is inclusive of others' vision and opening it up to scrutiny, through which wider possibilities of understanding can unfold. As Johns (2004: 205) notes, 'Fundamental to dialogue is to listen.' It is therefore important that the reflective dialogue is understood as such by its participants, for it would be easy to lapse into a power relationship communication which is potentially to the detriment of all concerned. Johns cites the work of Isaacs (1993: 24–5) to reinforce this: 'Unfortunately, most forms of organizational conversation, particularly around tough, complex, or challenging issues, lapse into debate (the root of which means "to beat down"). In debate one side wins and another loses; both parties maintain their certainties, and both suppress deeper inquiry.'

In the health, social care and education professions, culturally there has always been an element of debate – be it in education or in practice. The regulatory bodies insist on prescribing what is right and what is not. Given their statutory role, this is no surprise, and to some degree it is appropriate and necessary. However, it leaves a problem with how effective reflective conversations can take place in hierarchic organisational and cultural systems. Arguably, reflection is seen as a 'good thing' to be encouraged by these bodies, but only if it is evident that one person is learning from another who has greater authority and knowledge. This can be seen most clearly in the relationship that exists between students and their placement supervisors or practice teachers, where reflection forms a key component for learning, but also forms a component of judgement of competency. The supervisor therefore plays a dual role: reflective facilitator *and* assessor. Whether these two roles are necessarily compatible in a truly reflective dialogue is (to use one of our earlier terms) debatable, for if I am to reflect on how I see some aspect of care, as a student I may reflect upon it in a 'What do they want to hear?' sense rather than that which I find most troublesome or interesting. To have a real dialogue, as Johns (2004) suggests, we must be able to listen, and to listen carefully rather than to have pre-ordained assumptions as to what we wish to hear, or in ways that distort what we hear in order to fit into a particular scheme of thinking. Listening to service users, whether patients, clients or children, is, Johns suggests, far simpler than listening to and having dialogue with colleagues, for different forms of relationship exist within the communication space. They are less concerned with power and agendas, and more concerned with empowerment. Culturally, this is not necessarily so within organisations, and forms of communication which promote this may be considered subversive.

However, these issues should not be considered insurmountable. Johns and McCormack (2002) identify the environments in which reflection may flourish or flounder. Given that most guided reflection in existence in nursing, for example, consists of a model of clinical supervision, Johns and McCormack explore how this relationship can be equalised. This concentrates on two key points: first, a mutual understanding of what desirable practice is; and second, the changed perspective of monitoring as a responsibility of the self rather than of others. This second point is designed to move away from the construct of monitoring as a supervisory mechanism and one of judgement of performance to one of individual transformation and developing responsibility. In this way the reflective dialogue is equalised rather than being a method of surveillance, becoming a process of learning and self-assessment of effectiveness. In effect, it means a 'letting go' (Johns and McCormack, 2002) of traditional hierarchies and outcome-orientated activities and moving towards entering into the learning experience. Ultimately, in order to engage effectively in a reflective conversation of whatever shape or form, there needs to be an organisational system which allows this to occur.

Reflexivity

Finlay and McGough (2003: ix) note that, etymologically, the root of the word 'reflexive' means 'to bend back upon oneself', indicating that in research terms there is a consideration of the kinds of dynamics that can exist intersubjectively between the researched and the researcher, focusing particularly on matters of critical reflection around the researcher's social background, assumptions made, and behavioural impact upon the research process. Shulamit Reinharz (1997) gives an excellent example of what Finlay and McGough mean in her central question of 'Who am I?' while in the research field. For Reinharz (1997: 5), a number of selves exist in fieldwork, which have been broadly categorised from her own observations of self as an anthropologist:

- *Research-based selves*: being sponsored (removing myself from the sponsor), being a researcher, being a good listener, being a person who has given feedback, being a person who is leaving.
- *Brought selves*: being a mother, having relatives, being a woman, being a wife, being an American, being a Jew, being an academic, being 33 years old, being a dance enthusiast, being a daughter.
- *Situationally created selves*: being a resident ('temporary member', not true member), being a worker, being a friend, being a psychologist/social worker, being chronically exhausted, sick, and sometimes injured.

In different and fluid ways, Reinharz constructs a picture of the impact of self in any research process and findings. Her role as a researcher and loyalties to funders/sponsors as the audience of her research, her gender, gender roles, cultural and religious upbringing, and the context to which she brings this unconscious luggage will all contrive to see that which she is observing from a particular view. In her case, living within a kibbutz for a year brings challenges of familiarity and challenge, for she is familiar with Judaism, but is parted from her family and cultural signposts. If we transpose some of her background for other factors, the situation may be different: a single Spanish Catholic woman, for instance, would see the kibbutz through a different set of eyes. This does not mean that the study will have any less significance whoever conducts it, but the value of the reflexivity of the researcher will assist in sifting out the personal from the literal. The types of self that Reinharz creates are generalised categories that can be applied to any setting. *What she finds out about herself* will change depending on which culture she finds herself immersed in, and as a consequence the way in which the study is illuminated and progressed through will be from that perspective. As Reinharz (1997: 18) suggests, reflexivity is not about narcissistic display, nor is it a reaction to positivist thinking; rather, it is a balance between the objectivity of unreflexive positivism and subjective navel-gazing which enables the documentation of the self as a key fieldwork tool.

What is occurring, if we are to follow this pathway sociologically, are different experiences of symbolic interaction. First, there is that which can be observed as occurring in the world in front of us – the world of disability studies, for instance, has a wonderfully critical eye on how disability is constructed from a symbolic interactionist perspective. Then there is the second type – the symbolic interactionist occurrences between the self and the world viewed. All research is interactive to a greater or lesser extent, and it is through these interactions that a 'symbolic interactionist sensibility' emerges: that is, how the researcher sees what has been studied through their own lens, and how a reflective 'seeing of the self' is conveyed through the medium of that which has been studied.

A number of differing theoretical, philosophical and methodological traditions exist in reflexivity, including phenomenological, humanistic, psychoanalytic and feminist perspectives on self-knowledge. The variants of these traditions and the way in which the research is practised will inform the types of reflexive exploration undertaken, as Finlay and Gough (2003) note. These are likely to range between socio-political positions, social constructionism and postmodernism, depending on whether the approach is one of feminism, discourse and rhetoric, or ethnography. However, these can be categorised through particular general approaches, as Finlay (2003: 8–16) proposes through six constructs:

1   Reflexivity as introspection
2   Reflexivity as intersubjective reflection
3   Reflexivity as mutual collaboration
4   Reflexivity as social critique
5   Reflexivity as ironic deconstruction
6   Opportunities and challenges

Paraphrasing what Finlay suggests, the subject for research comes out of personal experience and an intense interest in it – an introspective self-dialogue – while the intersubjective element is translated as a critical gaze towards the emotional investment in the research relationships – a self-reflective consciousness that allows for a psychodynamic analysis of unconscious structure relations between participants in the research process. Reflexivity as mutual collaboration promotes cycles of mutual reflection and experience through participatory action research approaches, and, further, as a social critique exploring the power imbalance between researcher and participant through tensions which may arise as a result of different social positions, such as social class, race, gender, etc. Finlay (2003) cites Wasserfall (1997: 152) in stating 'the use of reflexivity during fieldwork can mute the distance and alienation built into conventional notions of "objectivity" or objectifying those who are studied. The research process becomes more mutual, as a strategy to deconstruct the author's authority.' In terms of reflexivity as ironic deconstruction, there is a consideration of the ambiguity of language, its meanings, its impact, and the ways in which these can represent the dynamics and multiple meanings of presentation. In this sense the ironic deconstruction refers to the potential rhetorical presentation of language between researcher and research participant which appear in paradox with each other.

From all of this, a number of opportunities and challenges emerge. In one way reflexivity can be thought of as a 'confessional account' of methodology (Finlay, 2003: 16) or an examination of personal unconscious responses to what is engaged in and found, and the way in which it impacts upon the self. In another, a critique of where the research is socially located and constituted is possible through deconstructing established forms of meaning. In essence, examinations of impact of position, rich insight and empowering through opening up a radical consciousness emerge as both the opportunities and challenges in reflexivity.

Conclusion

There is no doubting the overlapping qualities that are required to engage in effective reflection and action research. They can coexist alongside each other and simultaneously be embedded within each other as they are employed in daily working practices, but to be effective they require contexts which are transparent and supportive of allowing that which is unconscious to come into consciousness. This operates at both the personal and organisational levels, for neither approach is based on means–end reasoning, as Elliott (1991) describes above. It is more aligned with the notion of professional values and the effectiveness of practice in achieving what is valued. For organisational systems and individuals it is therefore deeply cyclical. Furthermore, the act of being reflexive is fundamental to effective reflection at a personal, professional and organisational level, for it enables crucial questions to be asked of self and identity within and of the organisation.

Bridget Somekh (2006) talks of the mediation of sense of self and identity in relation to data collection and analysis, and the interpretation placed upon this. This is perhaps the crucial differentiation which needs to be made between practices which are designed to serve different needs. She cites the work of Whitehead (1989) as proposing an exploration of the self and improvement of working practices being the core purpose of action research, which in her view creates an imbalance between that which can be weighted more heavily as professional development, and that which can constitute research. For her, the matter of self-inquiry in action research is one of research quality rather than one of professional development. Somekh (2006: 14) sees the self as a 'research instrument' subject to unique insights as to meaning making, but this is different to a reflective approach to improving one's own practice. The 'skill' of reflection is therefore transferable across these two forms of inquiry, but the purpose of its use is, for Somekh, discreetly different.

Action research in broad terms concerns the lived experiences of people and the understanding of the essences of reality. It therefore has two main thrusts: knowledge production through education and socio-political action; and empowerment through the process of people constructing and using their own knowledge. Methodologically, though, it is hard to pin down. Each inquiry is complex and unique, reliant on the people's roles in setting the agendas, participating in the data collection, and controlling the use of outcomes. Data collection is an evolutionary process, rather than being pre-determined (Winter and Munn-Giddings, 2001). The ideology of action research is one of collaboration, and, as Tandon (1989) points out, it is likely to sharpen people's capacity to conduct their own research and liberate minds for critical reflection within the existent framework of knowledge, and to uncover that which did not exist within their conscious frame of knowledge that can be used for their own purposes. Argyris et al. (1985) also describe this, but in differing ways. They see that, for participants, there is the consideration of reflecting not only on any action they may employ, but more deeply on the variables – the underlying assumptions that lie beyond the action strategy. Argyris and Schon (1974, cited in Reason, 1994) see this as 'double loop' learning – learning which refers to the capacity of individuals to consider and modify not just their action strategies, but the factors which govern their strategies. This is further refined by Torbert as a focus on the 'implicit cognitive models of practitioners and on their verbal actions' (cited in Reason, 1994: 330).

The reflective process can act upon these models and actions in both supportive and subversive ways, either through confirming what is understood theoretically and conceptually, or through raising questions – the paradoxical questions that emerge out of Finlay's (2003) notions of ironic deconstruction – which put these cognitive models and actions into doubt, and from which new and differing understandings emerge. These may be understanding of actions and thinking that refers to self, or of actions and thinking that refers to organisations or social structures. Importantly, as Sartre (1996) noted, one can immerse oneself in these forms of reflection and yet remain as a bystander to them, observing the process of reflection itself, teasing out the significance of certain elements of that which is reflected upon, which leads to new forms of knowing – not necessarily of a situation, but of our self. Weaving together the three discrete but overlapping constructs and practices of action research, reflection and reflexivity through recognising their inherent qualities is central to becoming a practitioner-researcher.

References

Argyris, C., Putnam, R. and Smith, M.C. (1985) *Action Science: Concepts, Methods and Skills for Research and Intervention.* Jossey-Bass. San Francisco

Argyris, C. and Schon, D. (1974) *Theory in Practice: Increasing Professional Effectiveness.* Jossey-Bass. San Francisco

Changeux, J.P. and Ricoeur, P. (2000) *What Makes Us Think?* Princeton University Press. Princeton

Elliott, J. (1991) *Action Research for Educational Change.* Open University Press. Milton Keynes

Finlay, L. (2003) The Reflexive Journey: Mapping Multiple Routes. In Finlay, L. and Gough, B., *Reflexivity: A Practical Guide for Researchers in Health and Social Sciences.* Blackwell Science. Oxford

Finlay, L. and Gough, B. (2003) *Reflexivity: A Practical Guide for Researchers in Health and Social Sciences.* Blackwell Science. Oxford

Ghaye, A. and Ghaye, K. (1998) *Teaching and Learning through Critical Reflective Practice.* David Fulton. London

Greenwood, D. and Levin, M. (1998) *Introduction to Action Research: Social Research for Social Change.* Sage. Thousand Oaks

Hegel, F. (1991) *Logic.* Oxford University Press. Oxford

Holstein, J.A. and Gubrium, J.A (1994) Phenomenology, Ethnomethodology, and Interpretive Practice. In Denzin, N.K. and Lincoln, Y.S., *Handbook of Qualitative Research.* Sage. London

Husserl, E. (1967) *Cartesian Meditations.* Martinuss Nijhoff. The Hague

Isaacs, W. (1993) *Taking Flight: Dialogue, Collective Thinking, and Organizational Learning.* Center for Organizational Learning's Dialogue Project, MIT. Cambridge, MA

Johns, C. (2004) *Becoming a Reflective Practitioner.* Blackwell. Oxford

Johns, C. and McCormack, B. (2002) Unfolding the Conditions Where the Transformative Potential of Guided Reflection (Clinical Supervision) Might

Flourish or Flounder. In Johns, C. and Freshwater, D., *Transforming Nursing Through Reflective Practice*. Blackwell Science. Oxford

MacNiff, J. (2003) *Action Research: Principles and Practice*. RoutledgeFalmer. London

Mercier, P. (2009) *Night Train to Lisbon*. Atlantic. London

Merleau-Ponty, M. (2003) *Phenomenology of Perception*. Routledge. London

Mezirow, J. *et al.* (1990) *Fostering Critical Reflection in Adulthood*. Jossey-Bass. San Francisco

Morton-Cooper, A. (2000) *Action Research in Health Care*. Blackwell Science. Oxford

Passmore, W. (2008) Action Research in the Workplace: The Socio-technical Perspective. In Reason, P. and Bradbury, H., *Handbook of Action Research*. Sage. London

Reason, P. (1994) Three Approaches to Participative Inquiry. In Denzin, N.K. and Lincoln, Y.S., *Handbook of Qualitative Research*. Sage. London

Reinharz, S. (1997) Who Am I? The Need for a Variety of Selves in the Field. In Hertz, R., *Reflexivity and Voice*. Sage. Thousand Oaks

Sartre, J.P. (1996) *Being and Nothingness*. Routledge. London

Schein, E.H. (2008) Clinical Inquiry/Research. In Reason, P. and Bradbury, H., *Handbook of Action Research*. Sage. London

Schon, D. (1983) *The Reflective Practitioner: How Professionals Think in Action*. Temple Smith. London

Schostak J. (1999) Action Research and the Point of Instant Change. *Educational Action Research*. 7(3): 399–418

Schutz, A. (1964) *Studies in Social Theory*. Martinus Nijhoff. The Hague

Schutz, A. (1970) *On Phenomenology and Social Relations*. University of Chicago Press. Chicago

Somekh, B. (2006) *Action Research: A Methodology for Change and Development*. Open University Press. Maidenhead

Tandon, R. (1989) Participatory Research and Social Transformance. *Convergence*. 21(2/3): 5–15

Wasserfall, R.R. (1997) Reflexivity, Feminism and Difference. In Hertz, R., *Reflexivity and Voice*. Sage. Thousand Oaks

Weil, S. (1999) Recreating Universities for 'Beyond the Stable State': From Dearingesque Systematic Control to Post-Dearing Systemic Learning and Inquiry. *Systems Research and Behavioural Science*. 16: 171–90

Whitehead, J. (1989) Creating a Living Educational Theory from Questions of the Kind, 'How Do I Improve My Practice?' *Cambridge Journal of Education*. 19(1): 41–52

Winter, R. (1989) *Learning from Experience: Principles and Practice in Action Research*. The Falmer Press. Lewes

Winter, R. and Munn-Giddings, C. (2001) *A Handbook for Action Research in Health and Social Care*. Routledge. London

Chapter 3

An overview of theories of consciousness and unconsciousness

He tries to understand me too well; he attempts to wheedle specific directions from me. He wants to discover my way and use that as his way also. Not yet does he understand that there is a my way and a your way, but that there is no 'the' way. And he does not ask for directions forthrightly but instead wheedles and pretends his wheedling is something else; he tries to persuade me that the revelation is essential to the process of our work, that it will help him talk, will make us more 'human' together, as though wallowing in muck together is what it means to be human! I try to teach him that lovers of truth do not fear stormy or dirty water. What we fear is shallow water!

(Yalom, 2005: 183)

Introduction

This chapter introduces some of the thinking around what we appear to know of ourselves, that which appears to remain hidden, and how what is hidden can become uncovered. As we have come to understand from the previous chapter, it is one thing to utilise a particular method, such as reflective practice, through which a greater appreciation of what we see and how it can be understood is gained; but it is another to develop a cognitive process through which this is enabled to happen. In this chapter I aim to explore some of the writing that has focused on both the physiological experiences and knowledge around consciousness, and some of the more philosophical discussions on how what exists in our unconscious is uncovered by us. Being able to operate in such a way is, for me, the key to real reflection. Arguably, in the health and social care and education professions, reflective practice has failed not because it is not useful, for I believe strongly that it is, but because it is seen as time consuming and of no practical utility to what is required. More purposefully, the tools supplied by the educators of 'learner' professionals (not necessarily students, for we are all 'lifelong learners') are not used to their real and full potential because they are reduced to superficial task-orientated processes. To use such tools, you need to know how to reflect before you can get the best from them; and because no one gets the best from them, organisations see no value in them. This results in non-reflective organisations: in essence, a 'non-reflective cycle'. It is to the conscious and the unconscious that we turn now.

Neuroscience, human nature and the brain

First, I want you to think about exactly who, or what, is in control of you. What dictates to you the actions you take? If you feel that you, what we call 'I', are in control, then Rita Carter (2002) would suggest that this is almost certainly an illusion. The brain, she further discusses, is subject to an ongoing assault by cues, such as waves of light, vibrations that ruffle the hairs of the cochlea, molecular bombardments upon the olfactory senses and nerve endings on the skin, and urgent messages travelling up the spinal cord. You may not be consciously aware of them, but they dictate what action is taken next. The most compelling cues, Carter suggests, are those which are most immediate, personal and odd. They capture our attention, and where attention goes, so does consciousness. We not only have a set of cues which are apparent in our environments, such as feelings of temperature, sound and physical aches and pains, but sensations of thought and emotions, and these combine to produce a fulsome mixture of experience. From this, Carter (2002: 12) asks three questions, paraphrased here, which set the scene before we delve into the world of the psyche:

1   Are you clear about the contents of your consciousness? Can you say, precisely, which things are conscious and which are not? At any precise moment would you say there were things that were in consciousness (such as this question) and things that – though known to you, like your middle name or the weather outside – are definitely not? In other words, do there seem to be two distinct levels of mind – conscious and unconscious – with a clear division between them?

2   How does it feel from moment to moment? Does your conscious-ness flow smoothly, continuously and in real time, or does it lurch along, interspersed with flashbacks, jumping backwards and forwards across images, or freeze-frames?

3   Lastly, whose is it, this sense of consciousness? It seems incontrovertible that your consciousness is yours. It is a single, private, unshareable world of your own, isn't it? Therefore, it is the most reliable source of knowledge that we have of ourselves, is it not?

Carter (2002) suggests that making such an assumption of our own consciousness will almost certainly be incorrect. It may be perceived that such an assumption is the most obvious conclusion that we can draw, given the nature of the question and the experience of our own consciousness. Yet, as Carter points out, we are the most unreliable of witnesses to our own consciousness, and even the assumption that our consciousness is our own private property is not as clear-cut as we might think.

One of the earliest thinkers on the subject of the unconscious was Eduard von Hartman, whose work began to appear in the late 1860s. This work, which became a foundation stone for psychology, began to explore the human condition of consciousness and unconsciousness both physiologically and philosophically. Drawing on the work of writers such as Immanuel Kant, his exploration of the unconscious included that which can be more visible, such as reflex action to external phenomena, and that which is less visible, such as whether ideas are always known to their creator. It is this area which is the first port of call.

> To have ideas, and yet not to be conscious of them – there seems to be a contradiction in that; for how can we know that we have them, if we are not conscious of them? Nevertheless, we may become aware indirectly that we have an idea, although we may not be directly cognizant of the same.
>
> (Kant, cited in von Hartman, 2002: 1)

Von Hartman (2002) goes on to discuss the notion of the 'unconscious idea' as paradoxical – for how can an idea exist if it is not in the consciousness? And if this is the case – if we can only be cognisant of the actual contents of our consciousness – then it follows that we can have no knowledge of anything outside of our consciousness. This leaves von Hartman with a problem: if it does not exist within our consciousness, then does it exist at all? Von Hartman feels initially that we can neither affirm nor refute that it exists, for until it enters into action, it cannot be measured as existing. Let us explore this for a moment. In a meeting to address a work problem, a colleague suddenly announces, 'I have an idea.' Where has this idea come from? Has it floated into the room and somehow journeyed into his brain? Or has it been dormant in his mind and suddenly emerged into his consciousness? We cannot know whether it has lain dormant, only that it has now become active. Yet the world is full of such statements as 'I have an idea' or 'Something has just occurred to me', implying an assumption that they do not exist prior to that moment. Delineating between conscious and unconscious thought can be tricky, but at the most simplistic level the example of Carter (2002) is useful, for she separates what is immediately in our consciousness from what is not. For instance, while I was writing this chapter, that was what was in my consciousness – the act of writing and reading. I was not conscious of my cat, so at that moment my cat did not exist in my consciousness. Then I hear her miaow and she walks into the room. Suddenly, she is now in my consciousness. It is not that she did not exist before in my consciousness; it is just that I was not conscious of her. In this sense, a thing becomes conscious through recall, sight, sound, smell, etc. I recently tried a little phenomenological study with a group of students. I gave them each an After Eight mint to smell, touch and ultimately eat. Each of them became conscious of something different through this, such as significant events, people or occasions in their life, or until that moment they had not wanted an After Eight mint to eat, but suddenly now they did. One who declined the offer of the mint said that she could feel and taste it in her mouth despite it not really being there – a kind of 'After Eight imprint'. One of the questions that emerges from this concerns brain matter, mind and consciousness, and whether what is occurring is organic, in a material sense, or of a perceptive or idealistic sort.

Edelman and Tononi (2000) discuss the issue of consciousness from the perspectives of science, psychology and philosophy, returning to the mind–body problem (dualism) as defined by René Descartes as a starting point. Descartes argued for absolute distinction between what is mental and material substance. Matter, he suggested, is susceptible to physical explanation, whereas the defining characteristic of mind is to be conscious – in effect, to think. From this, Edelman and Tononi explore some related ideas, such as epiphenomenalism, which is theoretically compatible with dualism in that mental and physical events of the brain are different, but which suggests that the only true causes of mental experiences are physical events, with 'mind' as a causally inefficacious by-product (Edelman and Tononi, 2000: 4). In other words, consciousness is related to bodily mechanisms as a product of the body's workings, and as such has no influence over the working of the body. In mechanical terms, this might relate to a car horn. The car is started, it creates an electrical charge, and the horn can be tooted, but the tooting of the horn has no influence on the running of the engine. Further, there is a field of thought which suggests that beyond the fact that there is a network and functionality of brain circuitry, nothing else is in need of explanation. It is fair to say that most roads towards resolving the problem of the substance of consciousness have remained unsolved, and ultimately a reversion to a 'science of the mind' through neurophysiology or cognitive psychology remains the dominant strategy.

This is not to say, however, that such matters are not up for discussion or contention. *What Makes Us Think?* (2000), by Jean-Pierre Changeux (a professor of neurobiology) and Paul Ricoeur (a hermeneutic philosopher), contains a whole dialogue between them which encompasses this debate. Changeux outlines two discourses that refer to two distinct methods of investigation into the sciences of the nervous system. The first concerns anatomy – the 'morphology' of the brain, the way in which it is microscopically organised, its nerve cells and synaptic connections. The second concerns behaviours, feelings, thoughts, emotions, conduct and actions in the environment. Out of this separation, he suggests, came the omission of the brain as researchable in the early part of the twentieth century, so that concentration on the observation of behaviour could occur, itself leading to an indispensable area of research in the neurosciences. In this way, behavioural data becomes the starting point when attempts are made to model cognitive processes.

However, this does not necessarily mean that neuroscientists partition particular forms of language, behaviour, etc. as sitting within certain anatomical areas of the brain. Changeux goes on to suggest that language, as an example, 'mobilises' areas of the brain in that it occurs through *'dynamic and transitory activities that occur throughout the neural network'* (Changeux and Ricoeur, 2000: 17). In other words, chemical and electrical activities enable an internal link between the concrete substance of an organisation of neurons, on the one hand, and the concrete measurement of behaviour, on the other. In this process, Changeux identifies a third discourse – that of *unity* – a functional dynamic which connects the anatomical to the behavioural through the neuronal response with that which is experienced or perceived.

This still leaves us with the problem of dualism, for whilst in operational form these ideas and theories seem substantive, it is the inclusion within this unity of thoughts, feelings and emotions which leads us to the problematic question of where personal experiences are 'housed'. The anatomical and behavioural constructs can be explained for Ricoeur (Changeux and Ricoeur, 2000: 18) as a category of objective knowledge – behaviour can be observed and scientifically described – and yet the question of personal experience, in which he refers to Georges Canguilhem's term 'vital values', is not so easily explained. In response, Changeux suggests, from a neuroscience view, that an individual's histories, memories and experiences accumulated over a lifetime are not the result of 'elusive metaphysics', but are given 'values' through a process of 'epigenetic signature stabilized in our patterns of cerebral organization and acquired by each person over the course of his or her life'. From this, Changeux adds that the fact that we are able to communicate our experiences in ways such as storytelling, art, poetry, etc. (something to which we will return in later chapters) indicates that although our brains are individually variable, they also give access to experiences as human beings that, although not necessarily very similar to our own, we can find agreement with. The neuroscience appreciation of this knowledge is partially constructed through advances in brain imaging, whereby experimental experiences can be objectively analysed and reproduced from one individual to another. An example of this lies in the use of positron emission tomography to observe the way in which the brain functions and responds to forms of stimuli, capturing visual data of changes in brain physiology in areas such as memory recall. Ricoeur counters the idea of epigenetic signature by suggesting that personal experiences depend on descriptions that have a criterion of significance through which they are subjected to an 'essential analysis' – 'something other' than an anatomical fact. Here Ricoeur alludes to a question posed by Edelman and Tononi (2000: 9): 'By what mysterious transformation would the firing of neurons located in a particular place in the brain or endowed with a particular biochemical property become subjective experience, while the firing of other neurons would not?'

In this field of inquiry many textbooks refer to the concept of the 'zombie'. A zombie is used as an illustration of a creature which looks, acts and speaks in exactly the same way as a human would. The one difference is that they are not conscious. Here, we need to consider that it would be a simple affair to describe a zombie's behaviour in terms of neuro-physiology, as it is incapable of having any sense of self. Edelman and Tononi (2000: 12) use this analogy to ask the question: 'What of ourselves? We emphatically are conscious . . . no amount of description can account for the occurrence of first-person, phenomenal experience.'

Similarly, the question of interpreting another's behaviour is a further dimension to this. Carter (2002) tracks the history of the concept of the mind, first through Descartes' likening of it to a hydraulic system, then, more recently, through thinking of it as a camera obscura, then as a telephone switchboard. Most recently, analogies are made with the computer – the brain as the hardware, the mind as the software, and sensation as input to the system. The brain becomes a 'central processing unit', a computational understanding metaphor that has been best applied by cognitive scientists. However, as Carter points out, this leaves a gaping hole in relation to consciousness, for if the brain is simply a computer of sorts, how does it know what it is doing, or the meaning of it? Where, exactly, is its understanding of this? Further, as Dennett (2001) suggests, a computer is neatly boundaried between the 'outside world' and the channels of information. Its internal and external connections are all integrated through a common medium – a pure signalling system which is not endowed with subtle feedback qualities. In the early twenty-first century we have computers of immense power, but they cannot negotiate their way through the simplest human interactions. They do not read facial expressions, do not know when it is appropriate to talk and when to be silent, are not capable of subtle forms of communication, such as listening and prompting, and cannot tell jokes or show empathy. They have no immersed connection to the 'outside world', and it is impossible to build a program such as this from scratch because of the sheer number of subtle demands and recognition of symbols needed to cope. To put the 'brain as a central processing unit' computer analogy into perspective, it is estimated that there are approximately 100 billion nerve cells within the brain. Around 30 billion exist in the cerebral cortex, which also contains in the region of 1 million billion connections or synapses. The possible number of neural circuits is estimated to approach 10 with a million zeros following it. By comparison, the number of particles in the known universe is roughly 10 followed by 79 zeros (Edelman and Tononi, 2000). And the brain is not much heavier than a laptop computer!

From this emerges a further question: 'Can there ever be a satisfactory scientific account of consciousness?' It is from this question that Edelman and Tononi (2000) outline the limitations of scientific method in this field, for, as they illustrate, science can provide the conditions which are necessary for a phenomenon to take place, can explain the properties of a phenomenon, and can explain the reasons why a phenomenon takes place under those conditions – a theoretical modelling if you will – but it cannot provide a substitute for the real thing. As such, they argue, whilst it may be possible to provide adequate descriptions of neural processes as corresponding to concepts of consciousness, that in itself is insufficient to experience it as it really is. For Edelman and Tononi, this is a real problem, for as conscious beings studying consciousness, scientists cannot objectively remove themselves from what is being studied, as they would with any other phenomenon – this in itself is a flaw in scientific methodology.

Bearing in mind what Georges Canguilhem says about science and research – that we only ever find out where we were wrong rather than where we were right – we can therefore only say of the brain and consciousness what *appears to be* the case. Edelman and Tononi (2000) conclude that, at present, conscious experience seems to be associated with a simultaneous distribution of neuronal activity across the different areas of the brain and neural groups. Therefore, they suggest it is not housed in one area, but rather the neural substrates of consciousness are spread across the thalamocortical system and its associated regions. In order for consciousness experience to be supported, a significant number of groups of neurons must react to each other rapidly and reciprocally through a process called re-entry. If something disrupts the re-entry process, such as interactions being blocked, then a degree of consciousness may disappear. Also, it is important that the neurons which are supporting consciousness as an experience must constantly change and differentiate themselves from one another, for if they all begin acting in the same way the neuronal repertoires of the brain are reduced, which can result in the disappearance of consciousness, such as is evident in deep sleep or some epileptic seizures – mainly of a generalised type, such as absence or tonic-clonic seizures.

Daniel Dennett (2001) takes the understanding of consciousness from a philosophy of neuroscience perspective and then begins to ask some questions of it: for instance, if the neuronal re-entry process is effectively one of sensitivity to (predominantly) the outside world, as Carter (2002) suggests above, then is it functioning as an 'intentional system' or as a 'genuine mind'? The question is one of enjoyment of sentience – (more or less) the standard term for what is imagined to be the lowest level of consciousness (Dennett, 2001: 84). Dennett argues that sensitivity requires no consciousness at all: photographic film is sensitive to light, thermostats are sensitive to environmental temperatures, domestic alarm systems are sensitive to movement, etc. There is a popular opinion, as Dennett points out, that plants and some lower forms of animal species, such as jellyfish, sponges, etc., are 'sensitive' without being sentient, but that 'higher' forms of animal, including humans, are equipped with sensitive capabilities of one sort or another but also with *sentience*. Dennett provides a lovely example of the complex degrees of functionalism that exist in 'sensitive' systems – from plant life, to machines, and through to humans – suggesting that sentience may exist in plants, but that it happens at a much slower rate than that experienced by humans. In other words, plants might have the capacity to think and consider as parts of their functional system through the same biological and chemical constructs that apply to humans, but it happens over such substantial time that we are incapable of seeing it as behaviour. This functionalism in humans, though, is clouded by knowing ourselves as existing within these functional systems.

Dennett's (2001) example of this is a mind/brain/body question, for the human 'system' as such is one of a series of organs working in collaboration with each other. If one is damaged, the others become affected. Now, some of these, such as the heart and the liver, can be artificially supported and even replaced through transplantation. At this point 'ownership' of organs becomes an issue, for if your heart were failing, you would probably be the happy recipient of another, should it be donated to you. But would you be the happy recipient of another brain into your body? After all, in a functional system approach, it is simply like transplanting a new engine into a car whose old one has gone 'bang', isn't it? Given the choice, you would probably be happier to donate your brain to someone else, for your mind would go with it. Of course, there is a further element to this, as Dennett points out: there cannot possibly be a clean cut to this because the mind/brain and body are intimately connected. To place a brain into another body would mean that it loses the talents, physical memories and capabilities that formed its identity of a 'self'. It may no longer have the capacity to play the violin, run 400 metres in under a minute, or paint watercolours, for it no longer has the dispositions that made it who it was. Put succinctly, if another brain were transplanted into your body, you would no longer be 'you'. And if your brain were transplanted into another body, you would still no longer be 'you'. In critiquing functionality, Dennett suggests that once we abandon the notion of the mind existing solely within the brain but as part of a non-insulated system held within the body itself (not just the nervous system, but in its entirety) we can recognise much of the 'wisdom' that is exploited in daily decision-making without our realisation that it is happening. 'Mind' is therefore something that exists across all systems of which our body is constituted. Dennett cites Friedrich Nietzsche's discussion on 'despisers of the body' to describe this:

> 'Body am I, and soul' – thus speaks the child. And why should one not speak like children? But awakened and knowing say: body am I entirely, and nothing else; and soul is only a word for something about the body.

> The body is a great reason, a plurality with one sense, a war and peace, a herd and a shepherd. An instrument of your body is also your little

reason, my brother, which you call 'spirit' – a little instrument and toy of your great reason . . . Behind your thoughts and feelings, my brother, there stands a mighty ruler, an unknown sage – whose name is self. In your body he dwells; he is your body. There is more reason in your body than in your best wisdom.

(Nietzsche, 1954: 146, cited in Dennett, 2001: 104)

Therefore, as Nietzsche and Dennett suggest, information is embodied, rather than contained in one place. It is perhaps that some parts of the system need to be in a position to make clearer and quicker discrimination between what is best policy at a given moment to ensure an ongoing future – degrees of sophistication that complement and secure the longevity of those gained over thousands of years of evolution.

Sentience, then, although still tricky to define, in essence discriminates between that which consists purely of sensitivity in its most functional sense – responses to light, temperature, etc. – and that which is able to make decisions based upon what it is sensitive to. This, however, seems inadequate when we approach the phenomenon of consciousness, for if 'the mind' exists as something embodied, then the body makes decisions irrespective of the mind all the time. The mind does not tell the body when to flush with embarrassment, when to cry and when to laugh, and to a greater extent it has no powers over these things. (V.S. Ramachandran (2005) devotes a chapter of his book to 'the Woman Who Died Laughing' – a discussion on a disorder of the limbic system.) Sentience itself, then, is an inadequate description of or criterion for consciousness because it is something more than organic responses to phenomena. Consciousness appears to manifest itself as an experience of being able to view the actions and decisions of its embodied self. We cannot possibly be conscious of everything at once, as Carter (2002) points out. It is not until something comes into our field of vision, thought or physical being (such as pain) that we become conscious of it. Things happen both in and around us that we remain blissfully unaware of until we are prompted to observe them through whatever functional or systemic means are necessary – visual, auditory, tactile, conceptual, etc. Once this occurs, the capacity to observe our responses becomes apparent; we are both in the consciousness itself and conscious of being in it.

This could be classified as a 'conscious space', which Changeux and Ricoeur (2000: 134) discuss from neuroscience and philosophical per-spectives. In neuroscience terms, this space may exist as a neural setting within the brain – not necessarily a 'place', but a default that exists across it – in which operations occur which are distinctly different to those which are carried out in the unconscious parts of the brain and nervous system. Changeux describes this as 'somehow inserted between the external world and the organism' in which a number of phenomena, such as intentions, goals and plans, exist and are referred to through constant interactions with systems of neurons. In this conscious space, he suggests, each person tacitly carries their history, remembrances, reconstituted experiences, social conventions, etc. Further, in this space narratives of events and moral judgements are experimented and hypothesised upon. Ricoeur views this construct from a phenomenological perspective. He discusses that space can be experienced through one's own body, itself an extension of the sense organs and which we feel through posture, movement, etc., but also through the bodily experience of enjoyment or suffering. A space is therefore a habitable one – a common space which we occupy and move within – and yet can be an objective one, in that once we grasp the abstract – that we can be 'here' while something goes on 'over there' – we are able to cross over between the private and common spaces. Ricoeur suggests that the neuroscience constructs of physical traces as stored in the brain, such as engrams, lesions, etc., are not necessarily distinct from the spatial phenomenology concept of being both everywhere and nowhere, but are closely related to it. What is interesting as Changeux and Ricoeur move their discussion along is a sense that any experimental work into the field of consciousness, identity or comprehension of the self and of others which occurs through neuroscience or cognitive psychology is a simplification of the phenomenon itself. It is inevitably reductionist and cannot account for variation. Consciousness itself will not be understood or represented fully by professions working independently, for instance by measuring behavioural or chemical responses to stimuli. It requires a much more collaborative approach, inclusive of cultural and social anthropology, neuroscience, philosophy and cognitive psychology.

The unconscious

It is impossible to do full justice to the work of neurobiologists and philosophers of neuroscience given the limitations of space in this book, but hopefully I have succeeded in providing some insight into how the field of consciousness is beginning to be understood. Now I wish to move on to some of the ideas that discuss the phenomenon of the unconscious. But before I do so, it is important to outline my thinking in relation to the nature of reflective and reflexive thinking, for it can be viewed from differing perspectives. On the one hand, reflective thinking, as was outlined in Chapter 2, is an important contribution to professional knowledge and competence, and there are examples of this in the work of Ghaye and Ghaye and others. On the other hand, reflection and reflexivity can explore that which is deeply personal, and through which new understandings of the self can emerge from the unconscious and into the conscious and which change approaches to aspects of life and work. Because the second half of this book moves into the affective domain through engaging in the arts and humanities, I wish to concentrate on the latter, and my way into this is through introducing some of the thinking behind psychoanalysis – in particular, but not exclusively, the work of Carl Jung.

Before engaging in the theory behind Jung's ideas, his work should be put into context. During Jung's lifetime, behaviourism was embraced as the general mode of inquiry, focusing on environmental causation for behaviour. Swimming against the tide, Jung's work aligned with a more current branch of animal behaviour biology known as ethology. Stevens (2001) notes that in this discipline, the focus is on the repertoire of behaviours which each animal species possesses. Accordingly, this repertoire is dependent on the evolutionary structures built into the central nervous system of each species, and these are primed to be activated when an appropriate stimulus is encountered in the environment. When this 'sign stimulus' occurs, the 'innate releasing mechanism' responds with a particular pattern of behaviour. The most obvious of these may be mating rituals. For Jung, this appeared as a pre-programmed mode of functioning as opposed to an inherited idea. Importantly, Jung (2005) saw this concept not to the exclusion of the environmental causation, but as a separation from the work of Freud on the notion of the 'personal psyche' – that at birth we are a clean slate to be worked upon – by the implication of a priori instincts which exist common to man and animals alike. These instincts, Jung argued, are universally distributed, impersonal, hereditary factors that often fail to reach consciousness (Jung expressly discussed this in psychotherapy terms, but my application is broader). According to him, these instincts are clearly delineated motivational forces that act without consciousness and pursue their inherent goals independent of any conscious activity. These 'patterns of instinctual behavior' (Jung, 2005: 44) are suggested by Jung to be archetypes of the unconscious images of the instincts themselves. What is inferred from the term 'image' is an expression not only of the activity and the form in which it takes place, but the situation in which the activity itself is released (Jung, 1998). The 'image' can best be defined as the human quality of the *primordial human 'being'* made real in specifically human form. In other words, Jung attempted to ascribe the qualities of humans through their primordial patterns to images of these patterns in a human form to which we could relate. These 'archetypes', as they became known, could therefore be archetypes of 'the mother' or 'the trickster' as examples illustrated in ways which could be related to, but grounded in instinctual and primordial human qualities.

Given this powerful archetypal structure, there has to be some sense of where they exist in relation to the psyche, and the significance of the psychic image. At this juncture, it is perhaps opportune to consider Jung's occupation with personal growth and transformation. Jung considers that human beings venture along a journey of lifetime development, and it is the recognition of the unconscious in us that will lead us to self-realisation – in his eyes a confrontation with the unconscious (Stevens, 2001). Indeed, in his autobiography, this is his first statement: 'My life is a story of the self-realisation of the unconscious' (Jung, 1995: 17). Making the unconscious manifest is for Jung both about freedom of expression, allowing the unconscious to produce itself, and the psyche to view itself and confront what it produces. In this process a split occurs between the conscious subject of the activity and the 'unconscious other' of the activity. The consequence of this type of thinking for Jung was one of heightened consciousness and the recognition of the psyche as a concrete, objective entity (Stevens, 2001).

Jung suggests that common to all of us are identical psychic structures that are part of human heritage. From this proposition, Jung sets out a series of foundational theories where in certain circumstances certain human responses are evoked which are of similar thoughts, feelings, images, myths and ideas, regardless of race, geography, class or period of history, and these form the basis for a collective unconscious which is responsible for integrating the whole personality – the self. In its simplest form, Jung suggests that it is the function of personal experience to 'develop what is already there'. In a sense, this means triggering or activating the archetypal potential already present, but latent, in the self.

It is important in the process of understanding Jung's thoughts that distinctions are made between different schema. Jung (2005) makes the point in *Archetypes and the Collective Unconscious* that the collective unconscious is different from a personal unconscious. For Jung, the personal unconscious owes its existence to personal experience, and is made up of contents that have at one time been conscious, but which have disappeared from consciousness through forgetting or repression. He describes these as the *feeling-toned complexes* that are constituted of the private and personal side of psychic life (Jung, 1998). The collective unconscious, on the other hand, has never been in consciousness and has never been individually acquired. For Jung, the contents of the collective unconscious owe their existence to heredity, and the 'collective' concept refers to the idea of embodied general characteristics of a thing, but which are implicit in their specific manifestations (Stevens, 2001). Similarly, archetypes combine the universal with the individual in that they are common to all human beings, but are individually peculiar to each person. Jung (2005: 42–3) describes this as follows:

> The concept of the archetype, which is an indispensible correlate of the idea of the collective unconscious, indicates the existence of definite forms in the psyche which seem present always and everywhere . . .

> In addition to our immediate consciousness, which is of a thoroughly personal nature and which we believe to be the only empirical psyche (even if we tack on the personal unconscious as an appendix) there exists a second psychic system of a collective, universal and impersonal nature which is identical in all individuals. This collective unconscious does not develop individually but is inherited. It consists of pre-existent forms, the archetypes, which can only become conscious secondarily and which give definite form to certain psychic contents.

Jung's thoughts can be broken down into some basic constructs which help in understanding his perspective: the stages of life; and the self and individuation.

The stages of life

Stevens (2001) notes that Jung held the belief that human beings were born pre-programmed with an elaborate system which was incorporated into the self and which presupposed the life-cycle of humanity. Within this there are two sets of specific components to the inner programme, each with different primary concerns. The first set are biological and social; the second cultural and spiritual. For Jung, this was identified through the natural aim of bearing and protecting children, and with this the acquisition of money and social position, and only when this aim is achieved does a new – cultural – aim become possible. In essence, Jung suggests that humans seek different qualities from these different stages of life, and those new aspects of the self become active and demand expression at the appropriate times.

The self and individuation

According to Stevens (2001), the self is both the architect and the builder of the structure that supports our psychic existence through our lifetime. For Jung, the goal of the self is wholeness and the realisation of the blueprint for existence in the life of the individual. Although these goals can be seen in biological terms, the self also seeks fulfilment in matters of spirituality, art and the inner life of the soul. Although archetypes exist within the self, they are linked to complexes that emerge out of the self. These include the ego, the persona and the shadow.

Rather than the ego being within our consciousness, Jung sees it as being at the centre of our consciousness. It is the ego that is responsible for our continuing identity as we progress through life, beginning in early childhood development and stretching through the transitions that are experienced as we grow older. Jung also suggests that it is only in the second phase of life, once the biological and social aims have been satisfied, that the ego and the self are able to confront each other in a transcendent function leading to higher consciousness.

The persona, just as the ego does, begins its formation in early childhood out of a need for conformity to the expectations of others – parents, teachers, peers, etc. Learning what is acceptable regarding attitudes and behaviours and discovering which of these are rewarded or punished facilitates a persona that builds in acceptable traits and keeps unacceptable ones repressed or hidden. For Jung, the development of the persona is one of codification of our self for the approval of others. Stevens (2001) sees the persona as a public relations expert deployed by the ego to ensure that people think well of us.

The third complex for consideration is the shadow. In this complex, Jung explores the inbuilt unconscious defence mechanisms of human beings, illustrating the differing responses of infants to their mothers and strangers, the former manifested in joy, the latter with wariness and withdrawal. The ability to distinguish between friend and foe and the predisposition to attachment from early onset are seen as biological patterns of behaviour, and for Jung the archetype of the enemy is one of the most important of all, and is actualised in the personal psyche through exposure to the social environment. There are two crucial elements to this shadow complex: cultural indoctrination and familial repression. Stevens (2001) suggests the qualities of the persona inevitably fall into the possession of the shadow – the shadow 'compensating' for the superficial characteristics of the persona, and the persona providing balance to the antisocial characteristics of the shadow. Jung saw the ongoing struggle to hide the shadow as a 'moral complex' which has its roots more in fear of abandonment and detachment from embedded cultural values than in fear of chastisement. Consequently, Stevens notes that a moral complex, as such, causes restraint of the shadow as a threat, and this leads to ego-defence mechanisms being employed to deny, repress and project experiences and feelings of 'badness' onto others in order that our own peace of mind is maintained. Unconsciously, then, we deny our own 'badness' and attribute it to others who can be blamed for it. This scapegoating may underlie the prejudices that we hold against groups other than our own. As Jung (2005: 284) says: 'The shadow personifies everything that the subject refuses to acknowledge about himself and yet is always thrusting itself upon him directly or indirectly – for instance inferior traits of character and other incompatible tendencies.'

On the subject of 'individuation', Jung says that the term is used to denote the process of becoming a 'psychological in-dividual'. Here he means that the person is a separate unity or 'whole' (Jung, 2005), including that which is unconscious. For Jung, this was a radical break from more traditional forms of psychology, where only the conscious forms the whole of the psychological individual – not least because, as we learned earlier, the conscious can be measured through what is observed in action whereas the unconscious cannot. Jung's argument is that if unconscious psychic processes exist, then they become part of the totality of the individual, even though they may not exist within the conscious ego. As such, opponents of this may deny that unconscious phenomena exist; however, Jung suggests that they are manifest in individual behaviour, and that consciousness is very far from explaining the psyche in its totality. He also suggests that there is no fundamental order to these phenomena. Unlike conscious phenomena which may be categorised and classified, unconscious phenomena are unsystematic, chaotic and without order. Jung cites dreams as examples, with their lack of systemisation characteristic of a lack of personal consciousness to place them in order. He also cites affective conditions – like joy and grief, love and hate – as opportunities for the ego and the unconscious to come together. For Jung (2005: 278), the 'autonomy of the unconscious' begins when there is a generation of emotion – instinctive, involuntary reactions disrupting the rational order of the conscious.

Second, Jung sees the process of individuation as one of destiny. Stevens (2001) cites a statement from Jung's *Collected Works* where this is explored from his biographical perspective: 'Individuation is an expression of that biological process – simple or complicated as the ease may be – by which every living thing becomes what it was destined to become from the beginning' (Adler *et al.*, 1953–78: xi, para. 144).

For Jung, individuation is more than just self-realisation; it is a biological principle. Central to the ideas of discovering one's true self, Jung felt that by overcoming our own parental and cultural beliefs, recognising and divesting ourselves of our persona, dropping our ego-defences, and rather than projecting aspects of our shadow on to others, we should come to know it and acknowledge it as part of our inner life. In so doing we will come to terms with personality that exists within the personal psyche, and conscious fulfilment of the intentions of the self (Stevens, 2001) – the integration of the whole personality. Similarly, von Franz (1978) sees the process of individuation as a real transformation only if the person is aware of it and makes a conscious connection with it, and can actively cooperate with it. Von Franz considers that we all, at some point, experience being part of some secret design over which we have little conscious autonomy. This 'psychic nucleus', as she describes it, can be effective only when the ego relinquishes its power claim to being the sole element of existence. This can occur only when the ego is able to listen to the 'inner urges for growth'. As von Franz (1978: 165) states:

> [I]n order to bring the individuation process into reality, one must surrender consciously to the power of the unconscious, instead of thinking in terms of what one should do, or of what is generally thought right, or of what usually happens. One must simply listen in order to learn what the inner totality – the Self – wants to do here and now in a particular situation.

Jung explored these ideas within himself as Personality No.1 and Personality No.2. The differences in the manifestations of these persona are evident in *Memories, Dreams, Reflections*. In this, Jung describes Personality No.1 as being constituent of all the qualities he was familiar with of himself that existed in the outside world. Jung describes Personality No.2 as the 'other' – an intensity of feeling and overpowering premonition that he could sometimes pass into, a state whose peace and quiet he sought. Rather than these being separate entities, Jung explains them as communicating through some kind of interplay, and says that room needed to be made to accommodate anything which could come from within (Jung, 1995).

Becoming conscious of the unconscious

There are ways that we can explore this process from different theoretical perspectives, or indeed as a combination of them, but in the main I will leave this until Part 2 of the book. For the moment, I would like to remain within the tradition of psychoanalysis, and Jung in particular, as a starting point. To begin with, I will concentrate on Jung's notion of the 'active imagination'.

Barbara Hannah (2001: 5) begins her chapter on the confrontation of the unconscious with the statement: 'The first point to establish for any reader who is not familiar with the psychology of C.G. Jung is that what we know of ourselves is not all that we are.' On the basis of this statement, she asks a number of questions as illustrations of this type of unknowing:

- Why might we miss a train we are apparently anxious to catch?
- Why do we do and say things we may regret afterwards?
- Why do we wake up depressed for no apparent reason, or wake up cheerfully for no reason that we are aware of?
- Why might we surprise ourselves by doing so much better than we ever expected of ourselves?

Jung set out to engage in the task of finding out the qualities which contribute to the known and the unknown, and Hannah (2001) notes his discovery of the technique that he called 'active imagination'.

In order to understand Jung's technique it is important to see what it grew out of in relation to the work of others. In the early part of his psychoanalytical life, Jung aligned himself with Freud's work on dream interpretation. In this work, Hannah (2001: 4) notes, 'he, like all the psychologists of the time, thought that when the analysis was over, the patient could keep in touch with the unconscious by understanding the dreams'. The use of symbolic language was applied to dreams to tell us something which we do not know, and which may be the last thing we would expect. However, Hannah says that, as Jung became confronted by many of his own dreams which he did not understand, he realised that the method was inadequate and began to search for something else. From this search he discovered the 'active imagination'.

So what is this 'active imagination'? Samuels (1999: 6) says it is a 'temporary suspension of ego control, a "dropping down" into the unconscious, and a careful notation of what one finds, whether by reflection or some kind of artistic self-expression'. Stevens (2001: 134) suggests that it is a 'technique for granting the psychic freedom and time to express itself spontaneously without the usual interference of the ego. It is the art of "letting things happen".' He then adds (Stevens, 2001: 135) that it is

> a state of reverie, halfway between sleeping and waking. It is like beginning to fall asleep but stopping short before consciousness is lost, and then remaining in that condition, and observing what occurs. It is important to record what has been experienced, so as to make lastingly available to consciousness: it can be written down, painted, modelled in clay, or even danced or acted.

In this sense, then, the act of active imagination must be to 'give up' temporarily one's sense of identity and allow the 'other' to flow into consciousness. In this model, it is the ego (identity) which controls what is allowed to be known and what is not. Once the ego is put to one side temporarily, then there is the potential for the unknown to emerge. As Stevens (2001) cites from Jung's *Collected Works* (Adler *et al.*, 1953–78: xiv, para. 125), 'In sleep fantasy takes the form of dreams. But in working life too, we continue to dream below the threshold of consciousness.' Stevens suggests that Jung sees that the soul acts in constant companionship with us, but we generally ignore what it has to say because we fail to hear it. It is through the act of active imagination that he perceives it can be rectified. Hannah (2001: 7) provides an example of this from her own experience. On discussing that the shadow is usually the first confrontation with the unconscious, and the notion that the more hostile we are to this form of unconscious, the more unbearable it gets, she notes that if one is accommodating to this – accepting its right to be as it is – then the unconscious changes:

> Once, when I had a dream of a shadow who was particularly especially obnoxious to me but from previous experience I was able to accept, Jung said to me, 'Now your consciousness is less bright but much wider. You know that you are an indisputably honest woman, you can also be dishonest. It might be disagreeable, but it is really a great gain.'
>
> The further we go, the more we realize that every widening of consciousness is indeed the greatest gain we can make.

The question that concerns us from the perspective of the use of active imagination within forms of action and arts based social research remains the one of its utility. What is it that separates active imagination as having potential as a methodological tool, as opposed to dream analysis, for instance? Hannah (2001) suggests it is more empirical and scientific in character, and as a method has a long tradition in man as a dialogue between eternal powers and coming to terms with them. In Jung's therapeutic terms, this suggests the uncovering of opposites that live within the unconscious and uniting them within ourselves. Salman (1999: 55) notes that Jung conceived the relationship between the ego and the remainder of the psyche to be one of continuous dialogue, a never-ending process within which the nature of the conversation is one of constant change. It is perhaps in the use of creative and symbolic unconscious material that these phenomena can be captured more clearly.

Salman (1999: 65) suggests that symbols emerge from the unconscious, and are not censored or distorted; nor are they signs for something else. They are, as Salman puts it, 'like living things, pregnant with meaning and capable of acting like transformers of psychic energy', before adding: 'Symbolic images are genuine transformers of psychic energy because a symbolic image evokes the totality of the archetype it reflects. Images evoke the aim and motivation of the instincts through the psychoid nature of the archetype.' Jung harnessed the symbolic images through active imagination processes, such as painting and drawing, and, as Salman describes it, once these expressions are 'in the bottle' a dialogue can be entered into much more easily.

Salman (1999) also notes that Jung believed there are two types of thinking, rational and non-rational, and within these constructs two different modes of information-processing take place. There is an imagistic, symbolising component to the mind which works by analogy and correspondence as opposed to rational explanation. Salman suggests that Jung's belief was that this type of thought was an indicator that it is predetermined to its archetypal origins – those patterns of behaviour and the unconscious that constitute the contingencies between man's history and the present. Drawing on mythological motifs and interpreting them in the light of modern dreams and fantasies, Jung developed the method of 'archetypal amplification'. In this the symbol is taken to have meaning grounded in the historicity of what is known about that symbol. So, for instance, Salman uses the symbol of 'the river' to connect the constructs of immersion, purification and dissolution. In mythology the river has an identity as a healer and as a sacred entity. Vannoy Adams (1999: 105), on the subject of imaginal psychology, and more specifically on the work of James Hillman, a colleague of Jung, suggests that for Hillman and Jung, unlike Freud, where the image is a symbol for something else, the image is precisely what it appears to be, and nothing else. In this instance, the psyche selects a particularly specific image from its catalogue of images available from the experience of the individual in order to serve a quite specific metaphorical purpose.

Imaginal psychology

Within imaginal psychology, the method encourages the individual into a proliferation of evocative images which enable descriptive qualities and implicit metaphors in adherence with particular phenomena. The images themselves, and the qualitative descriptions of them, therefore allow for elaborate metaphorical implications to be placed upon them. Vannoy Adams (1999: 105) suggests that this process is not simply inducing people to be more realistic, but to support the thinking that imagination is reality, and conversely that reality is imagination. In this notion what seems most literally real is in fact an image with potentially profound metaphorical implications. It is in this construct that the beginnings of the empirical and scientific methodology in the application of active imagination emerge.

There are a number of things which require some clarity in the process of active imagination. First, there may be no reference to, or derivation from, any object in the external reality with regard to the image itself – in fact, no such (or one) object may exist in the external reality. With regard to the discipline of imaginal psychology, Vannoy Adams (1999) cites Berry (1982: 57) who says, 'With imagination any question of object referent is irrelevant. The imaginal is quite real in its own way, but never "because" it corresponds to something outer.'

In imaginal psychology, it would appear that this lack of correspondence to the outer is not merely accepted, but welcomed, for it contributes to facts of human existence which cannot be eliminated. That is not to say that 'objects' do not constitute some part of this process. Vannoy Adams notes Jung's considerations on this when he comments, 'Ontologically the psychic image of an object is never exactly like the object' and, in epistemological terms, where subjective factors condition the image, they 'render a correct knowledge of the object extraordinarily difficult'. The image should not therefore be assumed to be identical within the object; more they are regarded as 'an image of the subjective relation to the object' (Adler *et al.*, 1953–78: vi, 472–3).

When relating the image to 'analysis', Vannoy Adams (1999) suggests that the purpose of analysis is the 'relativisation' of the ego by the imagination. In this process the ego is decentred – moved from the rather arrogant position where Jung has placed it, at the centre of the psyche, to one which is equal to other important images. (James Hillman feels that the ego itself is an image, and it is the relativisation process which decentres it.) In this approach the ego is seen to appear in dreams or active imagination as a whole, or at the centre of the psyche, when it is fundamentally only one part of it. It has to be noted that archetypal psychology of the type which Hillman advocates is rooted more firmly in phenomenology rather than any form of rigorous or systematic analysis. In order to demonstrate the relativity of all images, the ego is humbled through exposure to its prejudices and conceits. In this process, it is not the aim of analysis to integrate the psyche through compensation as Jung defines, but to create a relativisation of the ego through differentiation of the imagination. Vannoy Adams (1999) cites Hillman (1983: 17) in his view that the aim of the process is to debunk the pretensions of the ego, rather than to strengthen it. Generally speaking, Jung's emphasis is more clearly grounded in the compensatory nature of the unconscious, whilst Hillman is more concerned with weakening the position of the ego so that it is situated equally alongside the persona and shadow. In this sense it is less about active imagination facilitating the temporary suspension of ego control, and more about evening out the levels of importance within the overall archetype itself. Whichever way we choose to view this, it is the activity of 'freeing up' the ego so that it is able to allow in 'the other' that is crucial to this part of our discussion.

Although what is provided above is an introduction to some of the theoretical ideas as to how the process of coming to know oneself takes place, they are more imaginal descriptors than 'systematic' approaches. As yet we have not examined these ideas in any sort of functional way. If we are to assume that as images of the unconscious flow into conscious awareness the ego begins to participate in the experience, then, in so doing, Chodorow (1997: 10) notes that 'All the parts of an issue are laid out so that differences can be seen and resolved.' In terms of developing a model for this to occur through, Chodorow goes on to cite some examples that have been built on and developed by some Jungian authors.

First, von Franz (1980):

1   Empty the 'mad mind' of the ego.
2   Let an unconscious fantasy arise.
3   Give it some form of expression.
4   Ethical confrontation (added later was 'apply it to ordinary life').

Second, Dallett (1982):

1   Opening to the unconscious.
2   Giving it form.
3   Reaction to the ego.
4   Living it.

Finally, Johnson (1986):

1   The invitation (invite the unconscious).
2   The dialogue (dialogue and experience).
3   The values (add the ethical element).
4   The rituals (make it concrete with physical ritual).

Dallett (1982) cautions that this process is not as orderly as it might seem, and it is unlikely that such a schema would be followed in a logical fashion. As Chodorow (1997: 10) notes, there may be times when the various components interweave back and forth, or occur simultaneously. However, what is important is the mediating relationship between the image and the psychological development. Chodorow (1997: 12) suggests that this is the 'aesthetic way of formulation and the scientific way of understanding'. In active imagination a balance is required so that if the focus is too much on the image, the person may lose the goal of psychological development; conversely, if the focus weighs too heavily upon the analysis then the transformative power of the symbol is also lost. Chodorow (1997: 12) cites Henderson (1984): 'the important thing is to develop a self-reflective, psychological attitude that draws from both the aesthetic passion for beauty and the scientific passion to understand. The task is to express both, yet not be consumed by either.'

To summarise this briefly, Jung and other Jungian thinkers say that initially the conscious interferes in allowing the unconscious to emerge, stifling the opportunity to 'let things happen'. This 'letting things happen', where the irrational and incomprehensible of the unconscious become 'real', is the catalyst to the imaginal reality mentioned by authors such as James Hillman – the recognition that these images exist in some form of reality just as other material objects exist. As these images become 'archetypal', they become concrete entities upon which abstract themes can be developed.

References

Adler, G., Fordham, M. and Read, H. (eds) (1953–78) *The Collected Works of C.G. Jung*. Routledge. London

Berry, P. (1982) *Echo's Subtle Body: Contributions to an Archetypal Psychology*. Spring. Dallas

Carter, R. (2002) *Consciousness*. Weidenfeld and Nicolson. London

Changeux, J.P. and Ricoeur, P. (2000) *What Makes Us Think?* Princeton University Press. Princeton and Oxford.

Chodorow, J. (1997) *C.G. Jung: Jung on Active Imagination*. Routledge. London

Dallett, J. (1982) Active Imagination in Practice. In Stein, M., *Jungian Analysis*. Open Court. La Salle

Dennett, D.C. (2001) *Kinds of Minds: The Origins of Consciousness*. Phoenix. London

Edelman, G.M. and Tononi, G. (2000) *A Universe of Consciousness: How Matter Becomes Imagination*. Basic Books. New York

Hannah, B. (2001) *Encounters with the Soul: Active Imagination as Developed by C.G. Jung*. Chiron. Wilmette

Henderson, J.L. (1984) *Cultural Attitudes in Psychological Perspective*. Inner City. Toronto

Hillman, J. (1983) *Inter Views: Conversations with Laura Pozzo on Psychotherapy, Biography, Love, Soul, Dreams, Work, and the State of the Culture*. Harper and Row. New York

Johnson, R.A. (1986) *Inner Work: Using Dreams and Active Imagination for Personal Growth*. Harper and Row. San Francisco

Jung, C.G. (1995) *Memories, Dreams, Reflections*. Fontana Press. London

Jung, C.G. (1998) *Four Archetypes*. Routledge. London

Jung, C.G. (2005) *The Archetypes and the Collective Unconscious* (2nd edn). Routledge. London

Nietzsche, F. (1954) *Thus Spake Zarathustra*. Viking. New York

Ramachandran, V.S. (2005) *Phantoms in the Brain: Human Nature and the Architecture of the Mind*. Harper Perennial. London

Salman, S. (1999) The Creation of the Psyche: Jung's Major Contributions. In Young-Eisendrath, P. and Dawson, T., *The Cambridge Companion to Jung*. Cambridge University Press. Cambridge

Samuels, A. (1999) Jung and the Post-Jungians. In Young-Eisendrath, P. and Dawson, T., *The Cambridge Companion to Jung*. Cambridge University Press. Cambridge

Stevens, A. (2001) *Jung: A Very Short Introduction*. Oxford University Press. Oxford

Vannoy Adams, M. (1999) The Archetypal School. In Young-Eisendrath, P. and Dawson, T., *The Cambridge Companion to Jung*. Cambridge University Press. Cambridge

Von Franz, M.L. (1978) The Process of Individuation. In Jung, C.G., *Man and His Symbols*. Picador. London

Von Franz, M.L. (1980) On Active Imagination. In *Inward Journey: Art as Therapy*. Open Court. La Salle

Von Hartman, E. (2002) *The Philosophy of the Unconscious*. Living Time Press. London

Yalom, I.D. (2005) *When Nietzsche Wept*. Harper Perennial. New York

Part 2

Creativity and the practitioner-researcher

Prelude

Tao's working of things is vague and obscure.
Obscure! Oh vague!
In it are images.
Vague! Oh obscure!
In it are things.
Profound! Oh dark indeed!
In it is seed
Its seed is very truth.
In it is trustworthiness.
From the earliest Beginning until today
Its name is not without lacking
By which to fathom the Beginning of all things.
How do I know it is the Beginning of all things?
Through it!

(Lau Tzu, in Jung, 2005: 4)

Before beginning this second part of the book, I first want you to look at Figure 1. For the purposes of Part 2, I want to present it to you as a conceptual cornerstone that holds the whole piece together. How do we make sense of this image? What kinds of critical framework can we apply in the creation and decoding of such images and other media of diverse kinds which are consistent and which gain an understanding of being a reflective practitioner and a creative methodologist? These questions are vital in the development of a rigorous analytical model. We can also ponder the words of Lau Tzu's poem, some of which condense what is aimed at here perfectly:

In it are images.
Vague! Oh obscure! . . .

Figure 1 Student A

In it is seed
Its seed is very truth . . .
Its name is not without lacking
By which to fathom the Beginning of all things.
How do I know it is the Beginning of all things?
Through it!

Figure 1, taken from one of my students' work, is an example of the 'raw' data used to develop the ideas laid out over the next chapters, and it provides us with a focus – something which sets the scene. And the spirit of this book lies in the words of Lau Tzu's poem.

Chapter 4

What do we mean by creativity?

Introduction

> The key, in the end, is to reveal to students what is truly essential: the world of their own creation. What better gift could you make to a student than to render him sensitive to the art of invention – which is to say, self invention? All education should strive to help those receiving it to gain enough freedom in relation to works of art to themselves to become writers and artists.
>
> (Bayard, 2008: 184)

There are certain forms of communication which are deemed important, and this is irrespective of education, professionalism or research. More specifically, it is the forms in which *writing* is permissible, as students, as professionals and as researchers, that represents whether the communication has value – and this is further reinforced by reporting on what is observable or already known and established in written text. These texts are, in the vast majority, written *literally* as opposed to written in *literary* genres, and by this I mean that there is an insistence that professional, academic and research writing should remain objective and factual in order to be credible. And yet what is it that attracts us, and touches us at a human level, in art, literature and music that can in no way be matched by literal or factual text?

Anyone familiar with the film *Rain Man* will know the character 'Ray', played by Dustin Hoffman. Ray is an autistic savant. As such, he has near-genius capacity in calculating mathematical probability. Some real-life autistic savants have similar abilities in art, such as Stephen Wiltshire, who is well known for his detailed representations of complex cityscapes from memory; or in music, such as 'Martin', described in Oliver Sacks' *Musicophilia* (2008), who is unable to tie his shoelaces or calculate simple addition, yet can transpose any movement of a Beethoven symphony into any key.

Though highly developed in some areas, these people are unable to think abstractly, or to present their thoughts through complex forms of linguistics. In a sense, this is how we are expected to practise. As a product of our times, what matters to us professionally is that which is concrete. The current modern professional world is one which has difficulty in dealing in abstraction and linguistics, preferring the autistic savant world of *what is there* rather than *what might be*. This form of professional autism leads to those within professions feeling uncreative and unimaginative, and as such unable to engage with the notion of, or perceive themselves as, creative beings.

The epigraph from Bayard that opened this chapter is important because it provides the cornerstone for a new way of thinking about what is valid and the way it is communicated. It suggests that, as teachers, researchers and professionals, we can open up the ways in which communication takes place; and, as students, we can feel safe in representing ideas and feelings in ways other than the traditional and stifling forms of writing which currently govern what is acceptable and what is not. One might be forgiven for thinking that Pierre Bayard, as a professor of French literature in Paris, has a particular interest in creativity that differs from that of the scientific community, but this is not necessarily so. The physicist David Bohm (2004: 23) wrote passionately and with honesty about the creativity needed for scientific endeavour through the merging of art and science, and claimed that there will always be contamination of findings precisely because of the unavoidable involvement of the human psyche.

> [Indeed], no really creative transformation can possibly be effected by human beings, either in nature or in society, unless they are in the creative state of mind that is generally sensitive to the differences that always exist between the observed fact and any preconceived ideas, however noble, beautiful, and magnificent they may seem to be.

Bohm, like Bayard, whose emphasis is on how we uniquely interpret, construct and understand what we read (or, more accurately, do *not* read, in Bayard's case), saw self-knowledge and creativity as crucial in the scientific process. For Bohm, this process is beyond the purely mechanical, and any findings should provide consideration of the self and the ways in which the self may have influenced them, rather than make a smoke-and-mirrors attempt at objectivity. This brings us to a crucial question: What do we mean by 'creative methods'?

Because we are a language-based culture, perhaps our starting point should be with language itself. I will begin by discussing the work of Ronald Carter, who cites a passage (Carter, 2007: 24) by Margaret Boden (1994):

> Creativity is a puzzle, a paradox, some say a mystery. Inventors, scientists and artists rarely know how their ideas arise. They mention intuition, but cannot say how it works. Most psychologists cannot tell us much about it either. What's more, many people assume that there will never be a scientific theory of creativity – for how could science possibly explain fundamental novelties? And if all this were not daunting enough, the apparent unpredictability of creativity seems to outlaw any systematic explanation, whether scientific or historical.

Many texts have been written on the nature of creativity, but rather than focus on them in great detail I prefer to ground my discussion in examples of creative works developed by participants in my own work, so in that sense I make no apology for writing about what I consider creative methods. The nature of this book means that I can give no examples of performative creative methodologies, such as the way in which dance or ethnodrama or music and song can be used in a physical sense, so I have relied purely upon visual and literary forms of creative work. However, I feel it is important to differentiate between that which is *creative* and that which is *novel*. This is necessary because, whilst it may be applicable for a research problem to be approached creatively, it may not be appropriate to conduct a study which is 'novel'; for, whilst such an approach may be considered 'innovative', that does not mean it will be useful. By this I mean that the novelty should not trump the enrichment of the research itself, an idea that is reinforced in the work of Elliot Eisner (2008). In other words, whilst creative forms of research can be pursued, they should not lose focus of the utility of the method employed. If the novelty of the approach outstrips its utility, then it has served no purpose other than to be aesthetic. 'Novelty, or should I say "near novelty", is simply not going to be enough to sustain interest and engender high regard amongst our colleagues' (Eisner, 2008: 24).

Returning to Ronald Carter (2007) on this subject, he makes an interesting semantic link between creativity, originality and novelty. He suggests that there is a semantic connection between the words 'creative' and 'original' in that the act of creating, in many modern cultures, is invariably seen as new, novel and innovative, so whilst it is possible to be 'novel' in the use of arts based research, 'novelty' actually has two different meanings: simply new; and the type of 'novelty value' to which Eisner refers. Carter notes that in the late eighteenth- and early nineteenth-century Romantic period, the word 'creative' is linked to concepts of singularity and rarity in the way in which works of art are described. He then goes on to describe how contemporary views of creativity are connected to individual acts, and its resulting further associations with properties of the individual human mind. In this sense, he sees the link between human originality and creativity as being only a recent human development.

Eisner (2008) suggests that there should be equality between the utility of the research and its aesthetic qualities. In any arts based research there will be a desire to produce a 'work' which has aesthetic qualities – a sense of pleasing shape or form, or of words or music to which we are drawn – and to some degree the production of this work will promote understanding. Yet the work must also not lose sight of the world it is portraying, for we exist in a world of correspondence theory, where 'truths' (of a sort) have been gathered in particular forms of empirical ways, and it is a matter for consideration as to how the product of such research will be accepted by our colleagues. Eisner's point of departure – and mine, to a greater extent – is that we need multiple perspectives on what constitutes research, which do not aim to find 'a truth'. Eisner (2008: 22) wants 'multiple roads to multiple Romes. I don't think there is one destination that several roads will lead you to, but that there are, rather, multiple destinations which require multiple roads.' Being creative is therefore important, and as such the possibilities for research are endless; but the construction of such research methods should reflect an underpinning rigour, as they will end in failure if they do not.

Creativity, thinking and self-knowing

In my Christmas stocking, every year without fail, I receive a puzzle – a steel ball trapped inside a wooden frame that I have to get out, a series of steel rings that I have to separate, or a jumble of shapes that when pushed together in a certain way form another shape. In these puzzles I test things out, remove things, return them, and remember the steps I have taken to reach a current point, until at last a new shape emerges, or the rings separate, or the ball is liberated. Sometimes I am just lucky and the puzzle falls into place without any systematic endeavour (McIntosh, 2009). Perhaps this is part of the problem that Boden (1994) alludes to – the element of serendipity, luck, the unexplainable rather than the probable. In a way this book, and certainly this second part, is an example of this – a puzzle to be played with until a new shape emerges, for both the writer and the reader.

In relation to creativity and self-knowing, I would like to start with David Bohm (2004). His unique position as both a physicist and a philosophical thinker places him in an ideal position to consider the way in which self-knowing has been considered in science and art. Writing on the relationships of science and art, he first considers the science of psychology and its aims of self-knowledge, and the ways in which people adapt to be useful and productive members of a society. The issue here is that individuals increasingly feel a fragmentation of existence – living in societies that they do not understand and in which they are unable to lead meaningful and harmonious existences. It therefore becomes more difficult to generalise about self-knowing as many feel inadequate in adapting or adjusting to societal demands.

On art and self-knowledge, Bohm (2004) notes that many artists have tried to give shape and form to states of confusion, conflict and uncertainty in order that they can somehow be mastered. Whilst these may give some short-term respite as illusions, Bohm suggests that they are also inadequate methods for resolving these kinds of conflict, precisely because they are illusions. He suggests that conflict can be dealt with only by being aware of the full meaning of what is being thought and what is being done. In this sense, he sees science as a gateway as it provides factual information about brain structure, its physiology and function, and how the mind works. From this a person can develop an art of self-knowledge in which it is recognised that sensitivity to life and its experiences will always generate conflict and confusion. What Bohm refers to as art's role in this is one of *artistic spirit* and sensitive perception of the individual him- or herself and the phenomena of their own psyche. If we return to the earlier discussion of how practitioners appear to have lost a sense of creativity in current practice, it is perhaps because the false split between 'artistry' and 'science' has caused them to fall into a particular camp upon which professional power is generated. This is an illusion, for it can be clearly argued that scientists deal in abstraction whilst artists deal in the concrete, or 'what is there'. Furthermore, if it is art's role to represent phenomena in ways which we find interesting, illuminating or beautiful, then these experiences occur equally in science. As Bohm suggests, beauty is a common notion of a subjective response of man – a pleasurable experience of what appeals to his fancy – but these responses can also be applied to science and the theories it generates – their coherence, order and harmony, and the way in which they combine as a unified structure. They can be looked on then from two perspectives: first, that of beauty; and second, as a means to understanding the basic facts of science, with the goal of ultimately assimilating them into a 'coherent totality' (Bohm, 2004: 39).

Creativity in the sense that I am trying to portray is an attempt at constructing ways in which coherent totality can be achieved through a collaboration between that which is created through diverse forms of artistic media and the theoretical ideas which can be layered upon that which is created. And like a scientific theory, it is constantly subject to further development, for it can never be considered 'true', as 'truth' – in both scientific and philosophical meaning – ensures that further investigation is limited. What is important – indeed vital – is that whatever is formed has a coherence that is 'true to itself' (Bohm, 2004).

The question of truth and its connection to creativity can be further explored by including concepts of the imagination. Richard Kearney's (1991, 1994) overview of the history of Western thought on imagination provides much food for thought in moving these ideas on, and it is useful to cite his work as a stepping stone for further inquiry:

> I would like to identify three main questions which guide my inquiry throughout: (1) how does imagination relate to 'truth' – the epistemological question; (2) how does imagination relate to 'being' – the ontological question; (3) how does imagination relate to the 'other' – the ethical question. In seeking to respond to these three general questions of the imagination, I hope to shed light on the more general question of what it means to exist in this world at the present point of time and space.
>
> (Kearney, 1991: 10)

Let us therefore explore imagination as the basis for human creativity and of our being in the world. It is also prudent at this point to re-establish the second dimension to this – that of the technical rationalist approaches to professional practices and the notion that empirical understanding is *the only* understanding that confirms the truth of phenomena. The work of Roy Bhaskar (1975) sets out an argument that suggests there is an ontological distinction between scientific laws and patterns of events, and this discussion forms the basis of a theoretical framework to discuss theories of science, both natural and social, in which constructs of imagination and aesthetics can take place. The influence of empiricism is therefore an important component for study and discussion, for the interdisciplinary nature of utilising an arts and science approach requires a sympathetic understanding of how these disciplines are worked on and displayed as a 'product', which leads me to reflect back to the nature of language and cognition (as discussed by Carter (2007), above) within these domains. This has particular relevance to the predominance of textual language as a means of communicating and understanding, and the notion of a meta-text or meta-language that enables meaning to take place in a way which is equally ontological, aesthetic and empirical. Whether aesthetics can provide part of this meta-text, or whether what can be constructed through aesthetics can be developed into a structural form through the development of new, or within existing, models, is part of this discussion.

One way of furthering this is through Daniel Dennett's view that things become conscious to us through a competitive process that takes place within our minds. Dennett (2001) argues that the human brain is like an echo chamber, storing and upgrading information, such as language, which allows us to recall, review and redesign our own activities. In extension to this, these mental contents become conscious to us by winning the competition against other mental contents for domination in the control of behaviour, and, as Dennett argues, we are 'talkers' and talking to ourselves is one of the ways in which mental content becomes influential and assumes a position in our 'language drive' (to use the computer analogy explored in Chapter 3). In relation to the unconscious and conscious, Kearney (1994) summarises the arguments put forward by Freud and Sartre by noting that for Freud the unconscious was a potential precipitating factor in the destruction of human civilisation, and for Sartre a denial of the human subject's freedom and responsibility because it remains buried beneath the surface of what is individually and collectively known and thus is not acknowledged to exist. In other words Sartre suggests that because there is no hard 'fact' of the existence of unconscious we cannot be held accountable for it, or indeed our actions as a result of it. He then examines structuralism and post-structuralism. In this work, he suggests, there is a celebration of the disclosure of an unconscious system of language as a force to unravel the humanist imagination understood as self-knowing entity. Using a statement of Jacques Lacan, he outlines that 'the unconscious is structured like a language' (Kearney, 1994: 256).

One of the ways in which we can examine the nature of the ontological and the aesthetic in this context is through the use of myth. Paul Feyerabend (1999) discusses the idea of myth as true account, and asks fundamental questions of the empiricist's understanding of myths through the recognition of the powerful forces that mythical structures can place on those believing in them, even though the evidence may be contradictory. Myths can then become true accounts of the universe, in agreement with what can be seen to be the facts. A myth can also be a fact until it becomes consigned to history. As noted earlier, Georges Canguilhem's (1988) work in the history of the human sciences asserts that we generally find where we were wrong rather than where we are right when furthering knowledge. This is echoed by the thoughts of others, such as Einstein, who saw their work merely as conjectures that would be superseded in the future. It could therefore be argued that we are ascribing a myth of truth to science because of the way it is located within our imagination and 'language drive'.

For Gaston Bachelard (1994), imagination creates illusions of reality and virtuality – concrete and symbolic meanings created by thoughts and dreams. Memories and images are associated, creating mutual deepening – what he calls a 'community' of memory and image. Ways of being are experienced through the threads of narratives and stories, and the connection between experience, memory and image is augmented through value. The image itself has value, otherwise it would not be kept as memory, and the memory is located within experiences of protection, comfort or anxiety, for instance. Memory and imagination have solidity in us, but the articulation of these phenomena provides us with challenges. Bachelard (1994: 6) uses the term 'psychological elasticity' of the image as a means for 'moving us at an imaginable depth'. In his book on imagework, Edgar (2004: 1) writes in his introduction:

> We are immersed in imagery. We have images of ourselves and images that we portray to the world. We rehearse future action and decision by imaging how things would be if we did this or that. We reflect on and evaluate the past through weighing up and sifting through our memories, just as with a set of old photographs. We can read intensity of mental image as compelling us to act, believe in ourselves in love or to be at one with the divine.

How we engage in this creatively, and in ways upon which these images become 'live', can occur through an arts based approach. The nature of the 'artistic spirit' as discussed by Bohm (2004) is something which Fish (1998) directs towards the caring professions. Fish discusses the idea that to enter into the traditions of the artistic paradigm, the (practitioner-) researcher does not need to produce real quality art, such as fiction or paintings. It is more important for them to have an interest in artistry, being willing to think like (or more like) an artist, attempting various portrayals of practice, themselves artistic investigations. It is not the quality of portrayals that is important, but the quality of insights across a number of drafts that capture practice, and the critical commentary applied to them. For Fish, it is the sketching process itself that enables the researcher to discover why a subject has made an impact, and to learn from or refine it. Sketchbooks often contain a number of attempts at capturing an element of the subject – part of the process of problem-solving and depiction. Portrayals of practice are not an exact matter of fact; they are more a capture of tone, feeling and spirit.

Fish (1998) suggests that to see professional practice as artistry is a means of seeing its entire character, and further suggests that professional practice is increasingly recognised in the context of artistry, and the practitioner is seen as a maker of meanings, utilising language that essentially comes from, and reflects a critical appreciation of, the arts. Fish splits this appreciation of the arts into two components: seeing and reading; and watching and listening. Using literature, painting and poetry as examples of medium, Fish explores storytelling, narration and imagery utilising a range of interpretive practices which form the basis of the language of appreciation with all its variations and subtleties. Within this framework, she argues that from this point we are able to explore meaning in, and formulate a response to, specific 'works of art'.

This response to art, not unreasonably, suggests that there must be a subject to appreciate it. In a professional context, this subject must come from practice. Fish (1998) focuses on the development of portraits of practice in words, seeing the production of narratives as draft portraits in conjunction with deliberations and reflective processes about them. Although these elements are intrinsically linked, they illustrate both practices and thoughts on practice, developing deeper and more reflexive understanding of procedural and propositional knowledge. In more detail, working drafts of one element may be necessary before refining them into a later painting. Key processes may require scrutiny of the drafts, a critical consideration of the artistry of professional practice, and an evaluation of the potential as the sketch evolves. Thus their evolution may need consultation to relevant theory to develop, or to be placed back within the context of the scene described, before any final portrayal of what has been seen and experienced is articulated. These working drawings are as important as the final portrait. They are the anatomy of practice.

Developing and refining these working drawings into holistic practices can then be seen as something organic, fluid, based on a jigsaw puzzle or theories of context, and, to return to the language of appreciation, can be seen from the viewpoints of portraiture (the process of adding to, layering or manipulating medium) or sculpture (traditionally the art of taking away materials, such as stone or marble, to reveal an object). Michelangelo's sketches illustrate this perfectly: parchments are scratched over and redrawn from various angles and perspectives using various materials, and he leaves notes upon the pages, messages to himself regarding technique and accuracy (see 'Anatomical Studies of a Leg' and 'Serving the Florentine Republic' in Hughes, 1997). Our appreciation of the subject therefore leads us through uncovering layers of knowledge and practices, revealing their meaning, or enables us to apply layers to the existing professional picture. For Fish (1998), it is significant that artists provide others with a means of seeing, and this is achieved through isolating and capturing interesting scenes, and accentuating the detail of these so that the interesting characteristics become clear. Edvard Munch talked of painting 'what he had seen, not what he sees' (Bischoff, 2000). In this sense he refers to the capturing of a moment that stretches beyond the physical composition, forcing an examination of interplays that would otherwise go unnoticed. These thoughts are echoed by Armstrong (1996: 77–8):

> In such ways the painter can draw our attention to features of the visible world which in our haste and habit we tend to miss; the painter does this not simply by noticing and recording, but by employing the resources of the art-form to make such visible phenomena more apparent than it would otherwise be.

So, what is creativity, exactly?

This *bringing into conscious* is something I wish to explore further by stepping back in time to some of the seminal work which has focused on the phenomenon of 'creativity'. Rollo May (1959: 57) asked a fundamental question: 'What is Creativity?' He attempts to distinguish between 'creativity as superficial experience' (aestheticism) and 'actual creativity': he defines the latter as 'bringing something new into birth' – the reality of something itself, as opposed to something which is merely an appearance or a 'frosting' to life. In essence this is the difference between something which is decorative and pretty, and that which represents reality itself. He makes a case supported by David Bohm – that any enduring description of creativity must not solely comprise 'works of art', but must be an explanation for the work of the scientist, the thinker and the technologist. It is, he suggests, the process of *making*, and of *bringing into being*.

In order for this 'bringing into being' to occur, there needs to be some sort of creative process. Carl Rogers (1959: 71) describes the creative process as one of 'emergence in action of a novel relational product, growing out of the uniqueness of the individual on the one hand, and the materials, events, people, or circumstances of his life on the other'. May (1959) outlines three stages in the creative process. The first is the *Encounter*. This is defined as a kind of discovery or confrontation – a discovery of a landscape and an absorption in it, or a scientific confrontation through an experiment – but it is not of an escapist sort, such as the decorative form described earlier. It is a discovery of a reality. Second, there is the *Intensity of the Encounter*, which is a heightened intensity of awareness, a heightened consciousness, where whomever is the discoverer becomes wholly engrossed in a state of creation. This does not mean that the individual is in this state only when 'at task', for there may be varying degrees of intensity that are not necessarily under conscious control. Those of us who have completed studies, written dissertations or conducted research will be familiar with the sudden emergence of an idea when we drift off to sleep at night or are driving to work. This is all part of the intense encounter. Third, there is *Encounter as Interrelating with World*. The question 'What is this encounter with?' becomes crucial. 'World' cannot merely be defined as the material world in which we appear to exist physically; it is more the pattern of meaningful relationships and the ways through which we participate, a cycle of world–self–world–self where neither can exist without the other. In this sense, May suggests that there is no such thing as a 'creative person'; we can speak only of a 'creative act'. In terms of the type of work I am proposing, this is vital, for it would be wrongheaded to suggest that creative methods are available only to those deemed 'creative', because it is not about the person. Rather, it is about the act and what is produced through it – a *process*, a *doing*.

More recently, Czikszentmihalyi (1997) has proposed that creativity – in line with Rogers' and May's thinking – is not a phenomenon that exists inside people's heads, but is captured in the interaction between their thoughts and a socio-cultural context. In other words it is a phenomenon which is inherently systemic rather than individual. Broadly speaking, this leads us to a construct by which what is constituted as 'creative' can be understood. Czikszentmihalyi (1997) refers to the original meaning of 'creativity' – that is, to bring into existence something which is genuinely new that has sufficiently substantial value to be added to the culture. The problem with this is that it is the culture which validates whether this new 'something' is genuinely new and therefore accepted into its fabric. It is therefore only 'creative' if it meets with the certitude of pre-ordained experts in its particular field, such as science, literature, art, etc. As part of an overall and fascinating discussion, Czikszentmihalyi does not ask what creativity is, but *where* it is. Leading on from the idea that creativity is socio-culturally located rather than personal, he constructs a systems model, for he suggests that in order to have effect, the idea must be presented in ways that are accessible to others, must meet the stringent criteria of experts in the field, and must be included within the cultural domain to which it belongs. To this end, he identifies that creativity can be observed only from within the interrelations of a system made up of three main parts.

He identifies the first of these parts as the *domain*, which consists of a set of symbolic rules and procedures that are constituents of symbolic knowledge shared by a particular society or by human beings as a whole. Obvious examples at both societal and wider human levels are birth and death, but others include music or dance. The second element of creativity is the *field* into which it is introduced. This acts as the gatekeeper for its acceptance or non-acceptance, so in the field of art the gatekeepers are art critics, collectors, teachers, curators, etc. In effect, a 'cultural body' – people charged with the maintenance of high culture – makes the decisions as to what deserves to be recognised, preserved and remembered. The third and final component in this system is the individual person. Creativity occurs when an individual, using the symbols within the given domain, sees a new pattern or idea emerge and applies it in such a way that it is selected for inclusion within the appropriate domain. This, in turn, is utilised by following generations or others in ways through which it evolves and grows, and through its followers it has an impact, for they in turn act upon it creatively. For Czikszentmihalyi, then, the creative person is not necessarily any different from any other; rather, the novelty that he or she produces is accepted for inclusion within that particular domain. Definitively, Czikszentmihalyi (1997: 28) suggests that:

> Creativity is any act, idea, or product that changes an existing domain, or that transforms an existing domain into a new one. And the definition of a creative person is: someone whose thoughts or actions change a domain, or establish a new domain. It is important to remember, however, that a domain cannot be changed without the explicit or implicit consent of a field responsible for it.

So what counts effectively is whether what is produced is accepted for inclusion in the domain, and although an individual may feel marvellously creative, if their view is not shared by the gatekeepers of the domain, their ideas will be deemed unoriginal or uncreative, adding nothing to the culture of that domain. Even having creative traits or talents, such as musical ability, or a gift for sculpture, or scientific endeavour, is not enough if they do not meet with what is acceptable for inclusion.

At this point we can begin to unite some of the constructs outlined above. For instance, we can see the relevance of May's (1959) three stages of creativity, and how an individual engages in a process of 'being creative'. We can also see how the issues discussed by Della Fish (1998) in relation to the practitioner-researcher – with regard to artistry, thinking more like an artist, and the powers exerted by technical rationalism – can founder upon the rocks of what the gatekeepers of the domain of professional caring deem appropriately creative, and therefore inclusive of that domain, and what they do not. Whilst Fish's work primarily relates to the caring professions it could equally apply to education and social science research, and so it currently remains on the margins, along with others of its type. If we refer back to Part 1 of this book and its concentration on the value of 'evidence' and what it is constituted of through a primarily positivistic approach, then the use of 'art' as a learning methodology and as a way of gathering and constructing knowledge may not necessarily be seen as 'creative' by the gatekeepers of the various domains to which they are applicable. To be creative is therefore not about plunging a domain into new and radical ways of seeing. As Czikszentmihalyi (1997) suggests, and as current utilisation of scientific theories illustrates, it is more an incremental process that builds on that which is already in existence within a domain. That it can occur through the use and application of arts based media is of real value, but if it is to happen it must be constructed within, and have appreciation of the scaffolding upon which the current domain exists. Therefore, in order to act with a greater application of 'artistry', it is necessary for individuals to surmount a number of obstacles in the way of being creative. They need to have a number of strategies which ease this path. One of the first major obstacles to overcome is the feeling of being 'uncreative'.

I now want to introduce an image and an accompanying piece of text from a course that I run for health professionals which focuses on using artistic media to develop reflective practice skills – 'Reflexivity in Professional Practice'.

These are two components of a portfolio produced by a student whom I shall refer to as Student B for the remainder of the book. They are the first in a series of images and prose which contribute to 'a work' necessary to complete a course of study, part of which is grounded in the use of artistic media, part of which is to construct a critical commentary which explores the development of their arts based portfolio. The author has deep concerns as to her creative ability. Her lack of creativity is a renowned

Figure 2 Student B

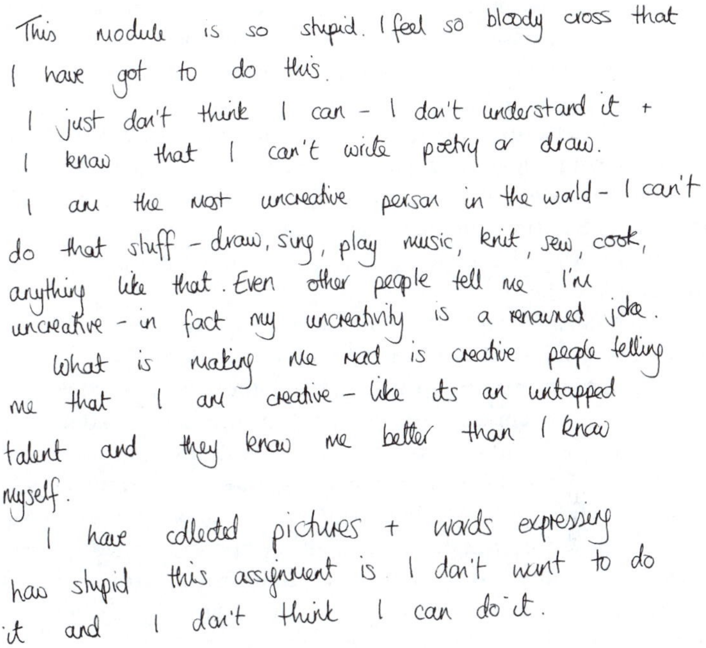

This module is so stupid. I feel so bloody cross that
I have got to do this.
    I just don't think I can - I don't understand it +
I know that I can't write poetry or draw.
    I am the most uncreative person in the world - I can't
do that stuff - draw, sing, play music, knit, sew, cook,
anything like that. Even other people tell me I'm
uncreative - in fact my uncreativity is a renowned joke.
    What is making me mad is creative people telling
me that I am creative - like its an untapped
talent and they know me better than I know
myself.
    I have collected pictures + words expressing
how stupid this assignment is. I don't want to do
it and I don't think I can do it.

Figure 3 Student B

joke, she says. She identifies herself as an uncreative being lacking in any artistic talent and so avoids any activity that she believes to be creative. In reflecting upon this matter, she feels she cannot put it strongly enough into words. In order to illustrate her depth of feeling, she produces the collage (Figure 2). This interesting and wonderful paradox in itself opens up a whole field of possibility – both for the author and for those such as myself who have a deep interest in this area – for how can a self-professed uncreative being suddenly produce such a simple yet effective medium of communication? I want to link this piece with some words from Czikszentmihalyi (1997: 344):

> Without access to a domain, and without the support of a field, a person may have no chance of recognition. Even though personal creativity may not lead to fame and fortune, it can do something that from the individual's point of view is even more important: make day-to-day experiences more vivid, more enjoyable, more rewarding.

When we live creatively, boredom is banished and every moment holds the promise of a fresh discovery. Whether or not these discoveries enrich the world beyond our personal lives, living creatively links us with the process of evolution.

Of course, some are more gifted than others in being able to portray and represent ideas and meanings. Their ability to use a pencil, oil paint, or sculpting tools may be something we can aspire to but are unlikely to achieve. Similarly, there are those who can structure words in vivid and authentic ways that we can only dream of, but this does not mean that they are the only beings who are 'creative'. What I see here in Czikszentmihalyi's words is a two-way process. Engaging in the creative act can, in itself, be rewarding for us; but so can the product of that act, for it has the potential to enrich the lives of others. Figures 2 and 3 create a sense of unrecognised possibility for both their author and a reader/viewer: for their author, a bringing into consciousness of what exists beneath; and for the reader, the recognition that creativity is not necessarily about brilliance, but about what it can bring to understanding. Whether it is considered of 'high quality' or 'limited quality' is irrelevant, because it is the substance within that we are seeking. Our first strategy, therefore, is to separate artistic talent from creativity. The second is to acquire and harness our creative energy.

At the most basic level, Czikszentmihalyi (1997) sees that to operate creatively is guided by external necessity – the actual time and energy available in our busy lives to devote to it – and internal protection – for, as was discussed in Chapter 3, the ego is constantly guarding against threats to the psyche. To free up creative energy, he suggests that we need to divert attention from the predictable goals that govern our minds, and use that which becomes available to explore the world around us – not just that which is evidently there, but that which *may be* there. Edward De Bono (1996: 87), for instance, talks of 'the creative pause'. In this pause, he says, '[I]f you do not pay attention to something, then you are unlikely to think about it. The creative pause is an interruption in the smooth flow of routine in order to pay deliberate attention at some point.' For De Bono, the creative pause is the simplest way to make a creative effort; it enables breaks in the flow of thinking, enabling a critical appreciation of that thinking, and allows an uncovering of ideas and patterns.

In taking a creative pause ourselves now, we can examine an example of a creative pause through the use of creativity by returning to Figures 2 and 3. For the author, there is a break in thinking that she is uncreative. Through the creation of the collage (Figure 2), she unwittingly breaks out of her seemingly uncreative world. It is not until the image appears in its fullness that this awareness takes place. She may not be 'an artist', but she has creative energy, and in being provided with a 'space' both physically and psychologically so that she can produce something concrete without threat to her psyche, something of great value occurs. To return to the work of Hannah (2001: 7) on Jung: 'It might be disagreeable, but it is really a great gain. The further we go, the more we realize that every widening of consciousness is indeed the greatest gain we can make.'

Some of us are by nature more curious than others, and some are more able, depending on personal circumstances, to drop their ego control and see what lies beneath. Being curious as a stand-alone activity is useful in developing our sense of creativity, but this, as Czikszentmihalyi (1997) realises, will be short-lived if it is not an enjoyable experience. Focusing our thoughts on whatever interests us in our lives, whether work or personal, setting goals for ourselves, enjoying what we do well are all things which can sustain our interest and enable creative pauses to take place. The creative pauses enable us to deepen the complexity of these interests and targets, which in turn become new challenges to our sense of knowing and being. These are forces of motivation which can be immensely creative properties when used to full effect; and it is possible that when beginning to have a greater degree of clarity regarding our personal traits and characteristics we will be able to 'author' our selves – within the boundaries of whatever we are: shy, quiet, exuberant, job role, etc. – through a kind of transformation and into a different kind of 'being'.

An example of this kind of transformation is presented on pages 102–5.

These images form part of a visual narrative presented by a nurse concerned with the ability of staff to engage in a clinical intervention, and the outdated state of the equipment used for this. Following a long period of inertia, she finally approached her newly appointed line manager, who suggested she conduct some research into the problem. To cut a long story short, she was ultimately asked to present her findings at a Hospital Trust Board meeting. Figures 4, 5 and 6 represent this. I will return to Figure 1 later.

Figure 4 is a representation of walking along the corridor to the meeting. The walls become narrower and more claustrophobic, and there is a fire in the room she is entering. Figure 5 is her view from the front of the room. There is a large table in front of her, and a series of eyes gaze at her. In the corner of the room there is a clock with both numbers and pound signs on its face. Figure 6 represents her feelings after the meeting – in which she has been told to resolve the problem and informed that whatever she requires as a resource will be made available to her. Although

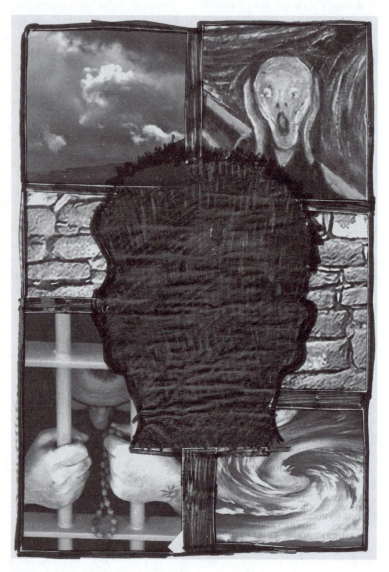

Figure 1 Student A

Figure 4 Student A

Figure 5 Student A

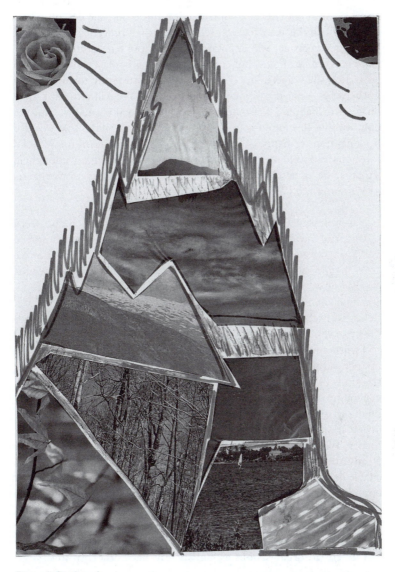

Figure 6 Student A

Figure 1 is presented as the first image in this series, it was the last she created, for in her critical commentary on this event, she describes how she lived with this issue for over ten years but felt powerless to resolve it until a new manager was appointed. It therefore felt natural for her to place it as the first frame, but conceptually it was her last realisation. As a postscript, she writes in her commentary of constructing the next image in the series – her fear of new-found freedom. We will return to these images in Chapter 5 for a more in-depth approach to analysis, but the point of this illustration is to demonstrate the possibilities that exist for personal transformation – for her sense of self and esteem transcended through the development of the images and the commentary upon them – that can be harnessed through the use of artistic media as creative pause.

Winter *et al.* (1999: 180) argue that

> as professional workers (and indeed as human beings), we possess a general capacity for effectively representing our experience in artistic form; we suggest that in order to realise our capacity for reflection we can (and should) draw upon our intuitive grasp of aesthetic processes as well as our capacity for conceptual and logical analysis.

Below is another example of creative endeavour, this time literary rather than visual.

I will come back to this work later in terms of its value. Here, however, in work of this type and others, such as those above, we need to consider the kinds of relationship that exist between artistic expression and the general processes of understanding. And, more importantly, given the theme of this chapter, we need to assess what artistic creativity and imagination enable in the learning process. Drawing on a broad range of theory, Winter *et al.* (1999) make links between the imagination and creative capacity. They identify two typical imaginative activities which enable its creative power. First, it reconciles qualities which appear to be opposite or discordant – through such schemata as analogy or metaphor – and plays with what is the same and what is different, and determines how this can be used to best effect. So, for instance, a school or a hospital can be described as a 'machine' (Morgan, 1993) or as an organism – much as I described organisations as 'autistic savants' earlier. In this sense, creative imagination is found not only in discovery but in everyday activity. Second, imagination is activated from within – the general is seen as particular, as meaningful and symbolic. What is imagined is in fact more than what is observed, used, or experienced: for instance, the equipment of a critical care unit in a hospital may be a monitor, a suction aid, a crash

Figure 7 Student C

trolley, but its symbolic nature is much more than this for those who use it or are the recipients of its use. When it comes down to the artistic creation from these imaginative activities, it is not solely that they *express* powerful emotions but that they *emerge from* them.

We can see in the work presented so far that there are transformative expressions – the work goes beyond that which it portrays. Interestingly, Winter *et al.* (1999) point out that this effect is particularly noticeable when the emotion is a negative one. Some time ago I attended a creative writing course, and my tutor Erica Wildwood professed that 'nice writes white'. In other words, happiness in literature is bland. It is much more engaging for the readers to immerse themselves in conflict and darkness, to engage in a conceptual and cognitive struggle before emerging out of the experience with a new feeling of consciousness. The images I present above are not 'cheerful'; they are representations of conflict which demand to be viewed and read.

At the same time, we could ask the question of all the 'imagery' presented thus far: OK, but is it any good as 'art'? Bearing in mind the comments of Czikszentmihalyi (1997), the gatekeepers of the humanities and the creative arts are ordinarily those who decide this on a grand scale, for they decide, as Winter *et al.* (1999) point out, which work is deservedly 'classic' and constructed by a true artist. Yet there is much 'art' in the public domain that could not be called 'classical', but is certainly popular – the amount of 'chick-lit' and crime fiction on the shelves of bookstores testifies to that. It would appear that 'art' in the current world is something which is provided to us by others who are skilled at something which is mysterious, to which we do not have access because of our perceived lack of talent. It is also something which we consume, as film, as music, as literature, as photography, etc. In this sense, these things become highly valued. As Winter *et al.* (1999: 209) suggest, 'Literature is simply "highly valued" writing.' Who, though, makes these value judgements? Is 'I Might Look Happy' (Figure 7) of any less value because it was created by a non-poet? Its value is in direct relation to the person valuing it. It may have no value, but it may also have immense value, so defining it in these terms is unsatisfactory as a conclusive ending. What is important is that these works have value in representing the capacity that exists in all of us for artistic creation. We may not only appreciate the established works that exist around us, and apply them in the way that Della Fish (1998) advocates, but also have the capacity to create works that are complex, carefully constructed, intricate and above all *useful* in developing and representing the ways in which we understand our experiences. As John Dewey (1958: 6) states: 'artistic creativity is an aspect of common human experience, in opposition to the "museum concept" of art'. Dewey goes on to describe the artistic structuring of such work – the making sense of its development; and this is true of those with whom I have engaged in this type of endeavour through workshops. They talk of 'an intellectual process' as the work comes into being: the way in which 'objects' are placed upon the paper or the page, the authenticity of the words used to describe, and what the images are designed to represent in the field of their professional reflections. Or, as Dewey (1958: 55) puts it more figuratively: 'It involves giving a form to experience which expresses its integration, its organisation . . . growth . . . development and fulfilment.' This is not just a matter of representing an experience in the way that a reflective model creates description; it is more a grasping of the whole experience itself – a more complete and intensified experience (Dewey, 1958: 45).

In the work of Barone (2008) we see how creativity can be polarised into big C and small c values, and the ways in which they impact upon others. Barone cites Gardner (2004: 45), who posits that 'Capital C change is the result of capital C creativity of capital C change agents.' For his purposes, this relates to examples from the arts and sciences, for instance Picasso, Einstein and Freud, and from public policy, such as de Gaulle – all major players in using creativity for change. At the other pole (small c) are those with a lower-case mindset – teachers, parents, those in the local community, etc. – who have direct responsibility for a 'mindful culture'. From this view, Gardner (2004: 132) credits Czikszentmihalyi (1994) in stating that while 'most of us cannot hope to effect big C creativity, we might at least expect to be "middle C creators"'.

The work presented as images above, and they are constructed in Dewey's and Winter *et al.*'s sense, fits within this concept of 'middle C creation', for it will not be distributed to the wider world as big C creativity is, but it has significant bearing when viewed from within its own field, and perhaps at a wider humanistic level. Czikszentmihalyi's (1994) term 'middle C creation' provides a marker for all that stems out of it (it is rather apt that middle C is also the central key on a piano), for it suggests that we have the requirements to create in such ways that can be of benefit to others without needing high degrees of talent to achieve our aims.

Conclusion

The notion of 'being creative' is in itself problematic, for assumptions can be made as to what it is based on from one's understanding of what 'creativity' means. A creative act can generally be assumed to be one of using the arts so that others can benefit from what is produced – a play or a painting to be enjoyed, for instance. Creativity is less understood as an act within experimental or theoretical science, or indeed in industry, but it is no less true that there are those in these fields who use the materials available to them and their knowledge of their subject to create something of use to others – a creation which emerges out of their knowledge, experience and imagination. Synthesising these two fields of creativity has been an aim of this chapter, bringing together the ways in which the creative arts and humanities can coexist alongside professional or social actions which are derived from practical and theoretical perspectives, and which lead to new ways of representing and understanding the experience.

Creativity and the tend to be perceived as having a primary role that centres on aesthetics, as discussed by Rollo May (1959) – a superficial experience through which we 'enjoy' or gain pleasure from that in which we engage. The 'actual creativity' he describes – the giving birth to something new – is more difficult to clarify. Indeed, when artists make such attempts to engage conceptually in their work they are often ridiculed as a result. (The Turner Prize in the UK is a good example, where often serious attempts at representations of experience are met with scorn in the popular media.)

Thus when we begin to examine the notion of creativity in relation to arts based research we need to consider it in the light of the theories that exist both in and around it: its production, its utility, its aesthetic quality, its 'novelty' both as innovation and as perceptions of 'novelty value' without substance. For instance, creativity would not exist if it were not for the capacity to imagine or visualise. For the purposes of research, it also relates to that which we experience, both internally and externally – both our inner and our material worlds in which we exist. It also relates to what is felt by those in power as to whether what is produced ticks the right boxes for that particular field and is therefore designated as a 'work of creativity', and this equally applies to individuals and how their actions set them apart as 'creative individuals'. It is fascinating that in the work presented in the images earlier, none of those individuals saw themselves as particularly reflective or creative. Yet, in the process of creating, an intellectual and reflective process took place which enabled the production of the work. It is not only the production of the work itself that is significant (it even could be argued that on its own it has little meaning), but what emerged from it – a sense of transformation. Whilst much of what is produced may not be considered by critics to be 'good art', that fact does not detract from its purpose, which is to generate new understanding of self and action through engagement in an intellectual and creative process.

As Eisner (2008) points out, arts based research must have utility beyond the aesthetic. In my view, it must also have value beyond means–end reasoning. It should not be used mechanistically, for instance as a data collection tool which is then discarded in favour of narrative. It is more methodological than that. In Chapter 5 I wish to take this further by exploring ways in which it can be developed methodologically, ways which are inclusive of analysis.

References

Armstrong, J. (1996) *Looking at Pictures: An Introduction to the Appreciation of Art*. Gerald Duckworth. London

Bachelard, G. (1994) *The Poetics of Space*. Beacon Press. Boston

Barone, T. (2008) How Arts-Based Research Can Change Minds. In Cahmann-Taylor, M. and Siegesmund, R., *Arts-Based Research in Education: Foundations for Practice*. Routledge. New York and London

Bayard, P. (2008) *How to Talk about Books You Haven't Read*. Granta Books. London

Bhaskar, R. (1975) *A Realist Theory of Science*. Leeds Books. Leeds

Bischoff, U. (2000) *Munch*. Taschen. London

Boden, M. (1994) *Dimensions of Creativity*. MIT Press. Cambridge, MA

Bohm, D. (2004) *On Creativity*. Routledge. London

Canguilhem, G. (1988) *Ideology and Rationality in the History of the Life Sciences*. MIT Press. Cambridge, MA

Carter, R. (2007) *Language and Creativity: The Art of Common Talk*. Routledge. London

Czikszentmihalyi, M. (1994) *The Evolving Self*. Harper Perennial. New York

Czikszentmihalyi, M. (1997) *Creativity: Flow and the Psychology of Discovery and Invention*. HarperCollins. New York

De Bono, E. (1996) *Serious Creativity*. HarperCollins Business. London

Dennett, D.C. (2001) *Kinds of Minds: The Origins of Consciousness*. Phoenix. London

Dewey, J. (1958) *Art as Experience*. Capricorn Books. New York

Edgar, I. (2004) *Guide to Imagework: Imagination Based Research Methods*. Routledge. London

Eisner, E. (2008) Persistent Tensions in Arts-Based Research. In Cahmann-Taylor, M. and Siegesmund, R., *Arts-Based Research in Education: Foundations for Practice*. Routledge. New York and London

Feyerabend, P. (1999) *Knowledge, Science, and Relativism*. Cambridge University Press. Cambridge

Fish, D. (1998) *Appreciating Practice in the Caring Professions: Refocusing Professional Development and Practitioner Research*. Butterworth Heinemann. Oxford

Gardner, H. (2004) *Changing Minds*. Harvard Business School Press. Boston

Hannah, B. (2001) *Encounters with the Soul: Active Imagination as Developed by C.G. Jung*. Chiron. Willmette

Hughes, A. (1997) *Michelangelo*. Phaidon Press. London

Jung, C.J. (2005) *Archetypes and the Collective Unconscious*. Routledge. London

Kearney, R. (1991) *Poetics of Imagining: From Husserl to Leotard*. HarperCollins Academic. London

Kearney, R. (1994) *The Wake of Imagination*. Routledge. London

May, R. (1959) The Nature of Creativity. In Anderson, H.H., *Creativity and Its Cultivation*. Harper & Row. New York

McIntosh, P. (2009) The Puzzle of Metaphor and Voice in Arts-Based Social Research. *International Journal of Social Research Methodology*, 99999:1 Published through iFirst, 09/06/09: http://dx.doi.org/10.1080/136455 70902969357

Morgan, G. (1993) *Imaginization: The Art of Creative Management*. Sage. Newbury Park, CA

Rogers, C. (1959) Toward a Theory of Creativity. In Anderson, H.H., *Creativity and Its Cultivation*. Harper & Row. New York

Sacks, O. (2008) *Musicophilia*. Picador. London

Winter, R., Buck, A. and Sobiechowska, P. (1999) *Professional Experience and the Investigative Imagination: The Art of Reflective Writing*. Routledge. London

Chapter 5

Using metaphor and symbolism as analysis

When I read a newspaper, listen to the radio or overhear what people are saying in the café, I often feel an aversion, even disgust at the same words written and spoken over and over – at the same time expressions, phrases and metaphors are repeated. And the worst is, when I listen to myself I have to admit that I too endlessly repeat the same things. They're so horribly frayed and threadbare, these words, worn out by constant overuse. Do they still have any meaning? Naturally words have a function; people act on them, they laugh and cry, they go left or right, the waiter brings the coffee or tea. But that's not what I want to ask. The question is: are they still an expression of thoughts? Or only effective sounds that drive people in one way or the other?

(Mercier, 2009: 25)

Metaphor

On first view, metaphor is simply a figure of speech, an embellishment of a concept that decorates language. But what is it that creates in us a need to talk in metaphor, either directly, through speech, or through other media, for instance through stories, film, songs or pictures? More importantly, what do these metaphors say about us? Can we classify them through some form of empirical process, and do they add to knowledge?

Before I get into ways in which metaphor can be used as analysis, it is useful to explore its roots and disciplines within historical and current thinking. It is also necessary to recognise the breadth of recent work on metaphor, and the application of that work. Metaphor has been considered in its application to learning and memory, but for the purposes of this work, its application is geared more towards usage, interpretation and impact, linguistically, visually and cognitively.

Metaphorical foundations

Paul Ricoeur (2003) identifies the work of Aristotle as significant in the development of metaphor. For Aristotle, Ricoeur notes, metaphor was made up of two elements: rhetoric and poetics. In this, public oration in Syracuse is described as a 'weapon' in that it is effective in serving a number of purposes. Focusing first on rhetoric, Aristotle identifies three areas: *inventio* (a theory of argumentation), *elecutio* (a theory of style) and *composition* (a theory of composition). The theory of argumentation is central to rhetoric in Aristotle's eyes, and because it has its roots in the invention of arguments and proofs it is fundamentally linked to demonstrative logic. Rhetoric, as a result, can be seen to be the careful consideration of public speech – its intentions to influence and eulogise, which when added to eloquence create the power of persuasion.

Poetics, however, takes us down a different road. Ricoeur (2003) feels that poetry is not dependent on rhetoric. It is not oratory and its aim is not to be persuasive. It is not grounded in defence or argumentation, but in representation and meaning. Although functional, poetics is concerned with the transfer of meanings of words and has the potential to articulate 'beingness' through analogy. In Umberto Eco's *Baudolino* (2003: 55), for instance, during a conversation between Baudolino and Niketas, Baudolino states, '[In] Paris you will study rhetoric and you will read the poets; rhetoric is the art of saying well that which may or may not be true, and it is the duty of poets to invent beautiful falsehoods.'

It is with these initial thoughts that Aristotle places metaphor with a foot in both of these camps, and Ricoeur (2003) suggests metaphor has a unique structure with two functions – a theoretical function and a poetic function. Metaphors in this view are used to argue, persuade and demonstrate through analogy.

Metaphorical scaffolding

Andrew Ortony (1998) connects these central ideas to the representation of reality, particularly the separation of metaphor from logical positivism and the driving forces that lead to beliefs in the use of literal language. In effect he identifies two paradigms – logical positivism and literal language – which create a powerful discourse when combined. Ortony discusses that under this precept, reality could be precisely described in ways that are unambiguous, clear and ultimately testable, and this leaves no room for the contamination of reality by rhetoric and poetics. The question Ortony asks is one of language constraint. He sees the verification of knowledge as being linked to cognition and perception. This relativist argument, he suggests, means that there is no foundation in a rigid differentiation between literal (scientific) language, perception, knowledge and other forms of language. These are therefore intertwined and impossible to separate. Furthermore, he suggests that at their most radical, two distinctions in conceptualising these types of language have been created: constructivism and non-constructivism, the latter being about the use of literal language only. Although he sees these distinctions at their most extreme, it is helpful to address the problem of metaphor within articulation of reality through these conceptualisations.

Similarly, Gibbs (1999) suggests that there are long-standing assumptions within the cognitive science community that cognition and language are independent of each other, and that the use of figurative language has little cognitive value of its own, being simply an embellishment of literal language. Gibbs cites the work of Lakoff (1990) in identifying two central philosophical commitments connected to literal meaning. First, *objectivist commitment*: in this view reality is made up of a system of objective and determinate constituents with properties and relations that connect those constituents at each moment. Most importantly, this view commits reality to a preferred description, and is a commitment to what reality is like. In this approach experiential reference points form the basis of what is 'true'. Second, the *Fregean commitment*: in this view, given the objectivist commitment to understand meaning in terms of reference and truth, the use of semantics is introduced. In this sense the relationships between symbols and the objective world, irrespective of the minds of any beings, are crucial. In this approach whatever is symbolic through experience, rather than any objective 'as it is' property, is important.

Gibbs (1999) discusses the idea that much of our thinking is structured as metaphor, as well as a significant proportion of our language. In editing the *Cambridge Handbook of Metaphor and Thought* (2008), he outlines a range of classifications as to how metaphor can be conceptualised: metaphor as mapping of thought, metaphor in language and culture, metaphor in reasoning and feeling, and metaphor in non-verbal expression. Because of the nature of these standpoints, it is inevitable that some conflict of thinking around metaphor exists between the most eminent writers in the field, and there is similar dispute over its limitations as a research method, for instance in the field of psychotherapy (see McMullen, 2008). However, at the most rudimentary level, and for my purposes, Gibbs (1999) suggests that metaphor underpins reasoning and imagination and how we think and conceptualise our experiences.

He argues that the language used for 'normal' contextualised knowledge and figurative language – traditionally seen as deviant or at best ornamental – does not exist because language is inextricably linked to our cognitive and physical systems. He seems to be suggesting that when we break down language the figurative component to it exists clearly, even when we attempt to be purely literal in our speech. Glendinning (1998: 93) discusses this further through an analysis of Derrida.

> [In the previous chapter] it was argued that the tendency to idealise the notion of 'meaning' is not something that it is possible simply or finally to bring to an end, as we might say, a recurrent logical fallacy. The 'prejudices' with which we are concerned here are not errors that are 'vestigial or accidental', 'rather (they are) a kind of structural lure' (Derrida, 1981, p. 33). The claim was that, while the idea of exactness does not actually play a role in the functioning of language, our language ceaselessly enjoins the ordinary speaker to presume its necessity. The philosophical urge to isolate ideal identities signified by words is, therefore, 'indestructible' (Derrida, 1988, p. 116) and yet it 'carries within it the destiny of its non-fulfilment' (Derrida, 1976, p. 206).

So where does this leave any sort of approach to an analysis of data where metaphor inherently exists, such as those presented in Chapter 4 (Figures 1–7)? Perhaps the most effective starting point is to ask two questions:

- What is metaphor? – The *nature of* metaphor itself.
- What is metaphor for? – The *use of* metaphor (Ortony, 1998).

Max Black (1998) provides some useful thoughts on the meaning of metaphor, the clarity under which metaphorical statements can make sense, and situations where nouns may just collide, making no sense at all. For Black, the concepts of *emphasis* and *resonance* are fundamental to a metaphorical classification. Although his work has been critiqued by writers such as Kittay (1987) in relation to his defining of the topic and vehicle of the metaphor with regard to the level of rigorous implication of language, his writing provides a good starting point in developing some ideas in how structures of metaphor can be applied to social research methodologies, and, for my purposes, visual and literary sources of data.

In more detail, Black (1998) uses the term *emphatic* to mean the degree to which the producer of the word allows variation or substitution for the words used. Where there is little or no room for variation, and where the metaphor or 'focus' – the salient word or expression – occurs in the literal frame, the metaphorical force for the utterance itself becomes apparent. In this sense, Black (1998) suggests there is discrimination between *dispensable metaphors*, which offer nothing more than oratory flourishes, and *emphatic metaphors*, which are intended to provide deliberation on unstated meanings and implications. In other words, emphatic metaphors have to be meaningful in systematic ways within speech. A relationship exists between the builder's perceptions of these pieces and how they become 'whole' to the hearer, and this is based not only on a systematic 'knowing' but on a 'feeling of the way' through that communicated.

The second area that Black (1998) identifies is *resonance*. In this view, the interpretive response to the metaphor will depend on the complexity and power of the metaphor-theme (the focus in question). The utterances that offer implicative elaboration (those that are most clearly identified by the receiver) to higher degrees are those that Black would see as resonant. A metaphor that is both markedly emphatic and resonant is therefore what Black would see as a strong metaphor, and he sets out a framework for how metaphorical statements work:

1   A metaphorical statement is made up of two discrete subjects, the primary subject and the secondary subject. The reference points to these are marked by the contrast between the metaphorical statement's focus (the word(s) that are used non-literally) and the literal frame in which it sits.

2   The secondary subject should be regarded as a system, rather than an individual thing.

3   The use of the metaphor works by projecting a set of associated implications upon the primary subject that are predictable of the secondary subject. This is what Black begins to refer to as the 'implicative complex'.

4   The author of the metaphorical statement works through a process of selection, emphasis, suppression and organisation of the primary subject by applying it to statements that have the same structure as the secondary subject's implicative complex.

5   Within particular metaphorical statements, the two subjects interact through the following schema:
    a   The use of the primary subject causes the hearer to select some of the secondary subject's properties.
    b   It invites the hearer to construct a parallel implication-complex that fits the primary subject.
    c   This induces parallel changes in the secondary subject.

Although Black uses the term 'subjects' as interacting, for his theory is one of interaction, he is referring in effect to the production of outcome within the minds of the speaker and hearer – what he refers to as the shift in the speaker's meaning, and in the corresponding hearer's meaning. Essentially this refers to what they both understand by the words used on each occasion.

This is important in terms of analysis. What Black (1998) suggests at an interactive level is a fundamental schema that places metaphor at the heart of communication. The non-literal word is used to create meaning within a literal system. It has a quality that allows these meanings to move from 'hidden' to 'exposed' within the literal system, and is reliant on the interpretive qualities of both the speaker and the hearer, and on their existing understanding of the phenomena in which the metaphor is applied. Both speaker and hearer therefore need to have an appreciation of the non-literal framing of the word and the literal system in which it is placed in order for it to make sense. This is echoed in the seminal work of Ferdinand de Saussure, as discussed by Jonathon Culler (1982). In this work, Saussure proposes that each language produces a distinct set of signifiers that coexist alongside what is signified, organising the world into concepts or categories. As an example, Culler (1982) uses the signifiers of '*riviere*' and '*fleuve*' in French, and 'river' and 'stream' in English, to describe this. What separates 'river' from 'stream' in English is size. Whereas in French a *fleuve* differs from a *riviere* not because it is larger necessarily, but because it flows into the sea. As such, they are not signifieds found within English, but represent a different articulation of a conceptual plane – that of flowing water. This could be applied further in the English language, for instance, whereby 'stream' can now be used as a description of money allocations ('budget streams') and children's academic attainment ('set streams'). These 'arbitrary' relationships occur, as Lakoff and Johnson (2003) suggest, through a systematic network of metaphorical linguistic expressions, and it is these linguistic expressions that can give ways of seeing into the metaphorical nature of our activities.

Lakoff and Johnson (2003) set out a series of systematic characteristics that support the identification of metaphorically defined concepts. In their view, the 'subject' can be understood differently from a number of conceptual metaphors, such as 'time is money', 'time is a moving object', etc. They suggest that it is possible for us to use expressions from one domain, and to talk about concepts in the metaphorically defined domain. They use the example of 'theories are buildings' to illustrate this, and examine how the metaphorical concept of 'theories are buildings' is used to structure the concept of 'theory'. Initially this is seen as being in relation to 'used' parts, for instance 'foundation' and the outer shell, and these are seen as part of the literal language about theories. However, there are also parts of this that are unused – such as 'the theory has thousands of little rooms and long, winding corridors' (Lakoff and Johnson, 2003: 53), or 'complex theories usually have something wrong with the plumbing'. Lakoff and Johnson suggest that literal expressions and imaginative or *figurative* expressions can be instances of the same general metaphor – in this case 'theories are buildings'. So, to continue the 'building' metaphor, extensions can be built on to what is already understood within the metaphorical conception of the 'object'.

From this basis, Lakoff and Johnson (2003) explore the use of the non-literal metaphor, and arrive at three distinct subspecies of this: first, extensions of the used part of the metaphor, such as 'here are the bricks and mortar of my theory'; second, instances of unused parts of the literal metaphor, such as 'his theory has thousands of little rooms and long winding corridors'; and third, instances of novel metaphor – which is a new way of thinking about something not normally used to structure part of our normal conceptual system – such as 'classical theories are patriarchs who father many children, most of whom fight incessantly'.

Lakoff and Johnson's (2003) ideas appear to correspond clearly with what Black (1998) has structured within his ideas of the 'implicative complex' – the selection, emphasis, suppression and organisation of the primary subject are applied to statements of the same structure as the secondary subject's implicative complex. However, Lakoff and Johnson add that there is a 'partial nature' to this metaphorical structuring, where metaphors can be part 'used' and part 'unused', and both used and unused parts need to be familiar with the receiver's understanding to work effectively.

When we begin to look at the communicative function of metaphor, Gibbs (1999) suggests there have been three traditional foci to its use:

- First, metaphors provide ways of expressing ideas that are challenging to produce using literal language (the inexpressibility hypothesis). Characteristics of thought such as 'swiftness' or 'suddenness' are hard to express in literal language, and even when we try to express these literally they still end up as essentially metaphorical: for instance 'a thought just entered my head'.
- The second function of metaphor is its use as a compactor of communication (the compactness hypothesis). This suggests that metaphor allows people to communicate complex information that captures the richness and continuity of experiences in a way that literal

language cannot. This is a matter of succinctness, and in many ways the metaphor acts as a scientific 'black box' where complex information is fed into one end through which it is reduced to comprehensible illustration when it emerges from the other.

- Finally, the use of metaphor may help to capture the vividness of an experience (the vividness hypothesis). Because metaphors have the capacity to convey complex configurations of, and are not confined to, discrete units, they allow speakers to convey richer, more vivid images of their subjective experiences, and consequently the listener is more likely to evoke various mental images that reflect the speaker's communication intentions.

An area that Gibbs (1999) highlights as particularly significant in the use of metaphor is that of emotion. On discussing a study carried out by Fainsilber and Ortony (1987), Gibbs finds that descriptions of more intense emotional states were described metaphorically more often than were those of less emotional intensity. This would support the 'vividness hypothesis' approach, and suggests that metaphor is more than just a linguistic embellishment. Indeed, Edgar (2004) writes that narrative embodies image, and that there is an inseparable dialogue and relationship between our understanding of the world as physical and cultural experience which in turn is made conscious through metaphorically structured language.

It is interesting to see where these metaphorical principles fit within other forms of thinking. Talbot (1995) looks at the role of fiction within language and social practice. She considers *text* and *discourse* as being opposed: 'text' referring to the observable materiality of a finished product, whether spoken or written; 'discourse' the process of interaction itself, a cultural activity. 'Text is the fabric in which discourse is manifested' (Talbot, 1995: 24). The analysis process in this sense is to look at the text itself, and at the interactions in which the text is located. In the same way that, for instance, Black (1998) identifies the 'subjects' as interacting, Talbot sees the process of text to discourse. It is both a product and a resource – a product of the writer/speaker and a resource for the hearer/reader. As a resource, text (which for my purposes also includes images) is made up of cues for the reader/hearer in terms of its interpretation.

Talbot (1995) suggests that lexico-grammatical realisations need to exist in text as a resource for the interpreter. For her purposes, three basic language meta-functions are inherent in any text: the ideational, interpersonal and textual functions. In a broad sense, the ideational function serves the function of language to create ideas and the relationships between those ideas – this is particularly relevant to content. The interpersonal function refers to the function of language and its capacity to establish, maintain and influence people. It considers social relationships and social identities. The textual function considers the text-creating function of language – the coherence between and the coherence of the various elements. The lexico-grammatical realisations or cues within the text are the encoded ideational and interpersonal meanings, and are interpreted and supported by other resources from outwith the text. In this sense, parts of the text are structural, whilst others are experiential. The text is not only on the page; it exists in the relationship with the other to whom it communicates.

Talbot's (1995) work focuses on the use of 'stories' and the fictionalising of accounts, arguing that there is a socially reproductive potential in fiction. In a sense, this is an echo of Michel Foucault's writing. Foucault (2002: 242) claims:

> There is nothing original in what I do. From this standpoint, what I say in my books can be verified or invalidated in the same way as any other book of history.
>
> In spite of that, the people who read me – particularly those who value what I do – often tell me with a laugh, 'You know very well that what you say is really just fiction.' I always reply, 'Of course, there's no question of it being anything else but fiction.'

Foucault's suggestion is that through the reading of these fictions there is both a connective and transformative component. In fiction, the act of reading involves us in an experience, and on completion of reading we have a different relationship with that subject than we did prior to the reading. Foucault's emphasis appears to be on the question of 'So what?' in relation to the interpretation of subject matter and its status as truth. And the figurative use of language in much of his work appears to be employed to create a system of relationships with the subject that may not have been achieved through literal language.

A further area for discussion is the use of spatiality in metaphor. Lakoff and Johnson (2003) consider the 'natural kinds of experience' form of defining metaphor. In this sense, experiences are a product of our bodies – including emotional characteristics, perception, motor capacities; of our interactions with the physical environment – such as objects, eating, our movement through the environment; and of our interactions with others within our cultures. Whilst these experiences are inherently related to 'human nature', they both produce and are a product of our internal and external spaces. For instance, the metaphor of 'journey' features heavily in language, and these journeys exist internally, externally, temporally and physically.

Anne Whiston Spirn (1998: 24) suggests that landscape metaphors have the ability to prompt ideas and actions and to modify perception, and that this in turn moulds the landscape itself. She describes it beautifully when she states: '[T]o know nature as a set of ideas, not a place, and landscape as the expression of actions and ideas in place not as abstraction or mere scenery promotes an understanding of landscape as continuum of meaning.' For Whiston Spirn, rivers reflect, clouds conceal, water purifies – meanings exude out of landscape features.

Tuan (2003) discusses the notion that a human being places a schema on space simply by their presence in the world. On most occasions, these schemas are not noticed, or are not made aware to that individual. Only when these schemas become misplaced are they noticed as absent. Let us explore Tuan's (2003: 36) description of becoming lost:

> What does it mean to be lost? I follow a path into the forest, stray from the path, and all of a sudden feel completely disorientated. Space is still organized in conformity with the sides of my body. There are regions to my front and back, my right and left, but they are not geared to external reference points and hence are quite useless. Front and back regions suddenly feel arbitrary, since I have no better reason to go forward than to go back. Let a flickering light appear behind a distant clump of trees. I remain lost in the sense that I still do not know where I am in the forest, but space has dramatically regained its structure. The flickering light has established a goal. As I move toward that goal, front and back, right and left, have resumed their meaning: I stride forward, am glad to have left the dark space behind, and make sure that I do not veer to the right or left.

Tuan's use of landscape not only describes the physical sense of being lost, but is a fine descriptor of the emotional sense of becoming lost, the internal uncertainty of our actions or thoughts when our reference points become unsettled. Descriptors of proximity – high, low, near, far, up, down – all locate us in a metaphorical position grounded in our relationship with the landscape. It is a spatial metaphor which exudes both *emphasis* and *resonance*.

Symbolism and dialogism – moving towards 'individuation'

If we accept that metaphor is a way of expressing meaning, then what is meant has symbolic value. Now I wish to move along a trajectory that brings together the use of metaphor, notions of unconscious to conscious thought, and the ways in which 'voices' can be constructed as they emerge out of what is uncovered through visual and literary creativity. Let us begin with a quote from Carl Jung (2005: 282):

> Normally the unconscious collaborates with the conscious without friction or disturbance, so that one is not even aware of its existence. But when an individual or a social group deviates too far from their instinctual foundations, they then experience the full impact of unconscious forces. The collaboration of the unconscious is intelligent and purposive, and even when it acts in opposition to consciousness its expression is still compensatory in an intelligent way, as if it were trying to restore the lost balance.

Jung (2005) goes further in this discussion to examine the nature of the relationship between conscious and unconscious. The failure for these two phenomena to make a 'whole' occurs, he suggests, as the result of an injury to or suppression of one or the other, causing an imbalance. If consciousness is the voice of 'reason' and unconsciousness the voice of 'chaos', then Jung argues that the conscious should be able to defend its reason, and that the unconscious should be able to have – as much as we are able to stand – its own way also. In this way both conflict and collaboration are able to occur at the same time, and from this an 'in-dividual' is formed. It is for Jung the harmonising of both types of data – 'the process or course of development arising out of the conflict between the two fundamental psychic facts' (Jung, 2005: 288). (NB: We have to remember here that Jung understood the 'soul' or psyche as no less a fact than any other physical object – as a realisation of psychic reality (Salman, 1999).)

Von Franz (1978), in a discussion of the progression of recurrent dreams as patterns, sees that symbolic interpretations are formed through the dreamer's conscious attitudes and these influence change over time. In this idea, in these dreams the patterns are related to increased senses of wholeness:

> Thus our dream life creates a meandering pattern in which individual strands or tendencies become visible, then vanish, then return again.

If one watches this meandering design over a long period of time, one can observe a sort of hidden regulating or directing tendency at work, creating a slow, imperceptible process of psychic growth – the process of individuation.

(Von Franz, 1978: 161)

Although von Franz discusses this specifically in relation to dreams, I would like to argue that these patterns become visible as 'fleeting glimpses' not necessarily as dreams, but in the engagement in life through representations and feelings. If this is the case, then it leaves me with a methodological problem in drawing these various strands together, for when is thinking merely 'dreaming' and when is it something more? Our minds are awash with 'memory images' which William James (1902, cited in Adler *et al.*, 1953–78: v) suggests are 'associative' trains of thought which influence each other, and are rooted in concreteness rather than abstraction. Reasoning, he argues, is *productive*; associative thinking is only *reproductive*.

If we look at the images presented in the previous chapter (Figures 1–7), they are grounded in symbolism. The work is not organised or systematic – it is arrived at chaotically, or, as von Franz suggests, it is meandered towards. It is not literal, for literalness would limit the interpretive capacity of it – literality would only make evident what is conscious rather than unconscious. Jung (in Adler *et al.*, 1953–78: v, 7) suggests that 'in modern speech we would say that the dream is a series of images which are apparently contradictory and meaningless, but that it contains material which yields a clear meaning when properly translated'.

Within this construct, Jung also looks at the way in which language becomes symbolic in its nature: when we are in moments of high intensity we talk to ourselves, or will draw images to make ourselves clear as a means towards *outward* expression – what Jung (in Adler *et al.*, 1953–78: v) terms 'directed thinking' – that first voicing of a new awareness. These sketches and utterances are symbolic representations of directed thinking that are resonant in the understanding of all of us. As Jung (in Adler *et al.*, 1953–78: v, 15) suggests: 'By this experimentation both thought and language are together advanced . . . Language grows, therefore, just as thought does, by never losing its synomic or dual reference, its meaning is both personal and social.'

Salman (1999) suggests that Jung understands the world as a unitary one, where there are inseparable relationships between interpersonal, intra-psychic and somatic phenomena, the analytical process, the world and life itself – destiny – much in the way that the physicist David Bohm (2004) sees that all matter is relatively connected. In the specific context of the nature of the ego and its relationship with the rest of the psyche, Jung felt that this was one of continuous dialogue (Salman, 1999), a never-ending process where what changes is the nature of the conversation. Each image in Chapter 4 is part of their creator's active imagination, not some random scribbling upon a page. The dialogue began before they put their mark to the paper, and we can see in the nature of the work the transformative tones of their thinking in action as the process of individuation begins.

In Jungian terms, this kind of analytic forms the basis of a method for 'archetypal amplification'. Here, I have built on the work of Edgar (2004) and his notion of 'image amplification' through the use of metaphor. For Edgar, a range of methods are employed essentially to make 'sense out of nonsense' (imagework) (Edgar, 2004: 81). These include such concepts as *symbol amplification* (dream re-entry). Edgar is very clear in his use of dream re-entry as part of a meditative imagining process – meditating upon a dream. For my purposes, there is no actual dream upon which to meditate; there is a process of examining fleeting glimpses of experiences upon which images are produced and a subsequent meditation upon those images. The images are symbolic and they can sometimes be amplified as dialogue on the images and the meaning themselves, and sometimes as dialogue on the thoughts produced in their development, such as changes in perspective of self. A further way of describing this could be to use Bachelard's (1994) term – the facilitation of 'psychological elasticity'. An illustration of this can be seen in Student A's critical commentary on her work, which is presented below the work itself (see p. 127).

Furthermore, the constructor of this image has sought out a framework around which to assemble her thinking, drawing on theories of transactional analysis to support her meditation on it. Creating the image triggered a necessity to explore theoretical ideas as a means to contextualise the feelings that emerged from it.

Dialogics

Having laid out some basic principles of metaphor, it is now useful to explore the nature of 'the voice' or 'multi-voicedness' in visual forms of data. One way of approaching this is through Mikhail Bakhtin's work on dialogism. A tension in the subject of dialogism is that although it was constructed by Bakhtin as a method that is different to the device of metaphor, for he was searching for a method to construct social

Figure 1 Student A

When anger or despair dominates reason, the *Child* is in control, at this time my internal reactions to an external event were making it impossible to make any rational plan to resolve the issue. I remained within this frame for over 10 years.

Further text accompanying the imagery expresses:

I realised that my Child and Parent Ego state continued to greatly affect my ability to explore beyond familiar social and working class boundaries. I retained beliefs that my position in society was one of subservience.

science systematically through analysis of language, dialogism can itself be understood as a metaphor, and this is an area for focus. Bakhtin's notion is that anything anybody ever says exists in response to things that have been said before and in anticipation of things that will be said in response. Therefore, we never speak in a vacuum. As a result, all language is dynamic, relational and capable of infinite re-descriptions of the world as we know it.

For Shotter and Billig (2003), the advocated approach is fundamentally one of uncovering the almost unnoticed events and features that exist in social practice. In this construct, it is the unfolding of the activities within which we relate to our surroundings and the responsiveness of ourselves to these features which are key, rather than the idea that there is a form of 'inner landscape' which we come to know. It is in these fleeting, unique discursive activities that we can begin to understand how the nature of our inner selves can be expressed to each other; what Bakhtin describes as the 'threshold'.

Gurevitch (2003) notes that Bakhtin considers the 'threshold' both as a turning point and as a moment of crisis. For him, it is not so much a matter of looking inwardly towards the self, as when the individual feels the pull towards the other, and where the nature of self can be expressed in that relational space. Gurevitch feels that the threshold should be regarded as actual reality, experienced and practised as a dialogical endeavour, symbolised through its characteristics of convening and dispersing, opening and closing, searching for common topics, silence and forms of speech. In essence, comparisons may be drawn between this articulation of phenomena, and that of image, where the image is seen as the concrete form of abstract themes. The threshold in this notion can be seen as having both discursive and sensory potential in how it becomes 'live' to the 'other'. To develop this notion further, Bakhtin (1984: 287) provides an example:

> Not that which takes place within, but that which takes place on the boundary between one's own and someone else's consciousness, on the threshold. And everything internal gravitates not toward self but is turned to the outside and dialogized, every internal experience ends up on the boundary, encounters another, and in this tension filled encounter lies its entire essence.

For our purposes, perhaps two kinds of threshold exist: that which emerges in the construction of the visual and literary data; and that which we are confronted by when we view the data from the perspective of 'the other'. Out of this comes a suggestion that there is a plurality – a latent plurality within consciousness – which can flourish within the 'dialogic' as an impassioned play of voices. For Bakhtin, this plurality within dialogics appears to be attacked from the sociological perspective; that is, the dialogic serves as a metaphor itself upon which the intersubjectivity of a society can be viewed and explored. However, the notion of selfhood and the way it both informs and is informed by the other is not excluded from the concept. Nealon (2003) discusses this by suggesting that the dialogic offers the opportunity to understand differences and ethical commitments without the requirement to fall upon a universalising or norm-giving structure in the way that other ontological schemes are constructed. The ethical dialogue then becomes one of social contexts rather than one of ethical rules. As Nealon (2003: 141) suggests, 'they open up a productive horizon to rethink the social landscape of self and other in our groundless postmodern landscape'. The suggestion is therefore that the terms of engagement in this process are found within the dialogics themselves. It is not until we are in them that the 'ground' – the ethical context – begins to emerge, and as a result this ground is not universal, but unique. A vital dialogic component, then, is our affective involvement in social practices and our capacity to 'read' the specific variables that can occur in both languaged and non-languaged activities with others. Carter (2007: 198) gives an example of this in his discussion on self-dramatisation through Bakhtin's concept of heteroglossia, where he suggests that both the narrator's and the character's voices 'have important intratextual relationships as well as intertextual ones'.

Perhaps at this point I need to be clear about what is meant by 'dialogue' and 'dialogism' from a Bakhtinian perspective. Vice (1997) suggests that the term 'dialogism' means double-voicedness. In this form, it is seen as both linguistic and novelistic in that it refers to particular instances of language in novels and in popular speech. The double-voicedness of dialogism is in the 'mixing of intentions of speaker and listener' (Vice, 1997: 45) – the positioning of utterances in relation to one another and in relation to creation of meaning. It is necessarily the way in which meaning is constructed. Dialogism is therefore a representation, whilst dialogue is an act of everyday activity – the conversation between two distinct subjects.

Differentiation of these concepts is indeed slippery, but for the purposes of this work I suggest that dialogism is related to the analytics that exist across relationships with and between those involved in the interaction – in this case, the creators of the images, myself, and you, the reader. What I mean by this is that the speaker can also be the listener to their self. If we consider the images as a set of utterances that are placed in relation to each other, then as well as placing those utterances, the creator begins to consider the creation of meaning, as I do in response to those utterances, and as you do in relation to my utterances. The context within this work of these particular utterances is more than merely a conveyance or construction of speech, more than a dialogue: it is engaging in the double-voicedness of dialogism.

In dialogism, consciousness is found in otherness. This is its conceptual location. Its role is one of multi-voicedness rather than one of self-centredness. However, this is not to say that the nature of multi-voicedness is not problematic in theoretical terms, for the threshold across which this dialogue occurs is built upon language, and to communicate one's intention one must have a sense of owning, or acquisition of, a language that belongs to oneself. Gurevitch (2003: 353) provides us with a statement from Bakhtin (1981) that explores this idea:

> The word in language is half someone else's. It becomes one's own only when the speaker populates it with his own intention, his own accent, when he appropriates the word, adapting it to his own semantic and expression intention. Prior to this moment of appropriation, the word does not exist in a neutral and impersonal language (it is not after all out of a dictionary that the speaker gets his words!) but rather it exists in other people's mouths, in other people's contexts, serving other people's intentions: it is from there that one must take the word and make it one's own.

We can return to Umberto Eco's *Baudolino* (2003: 13) for an illustration of this in a description of Niketas:

> But Niketas was curious by nature. He loved to listen to the stories of others, and not only those concerning things unknown to him. Even things he had seen with his own eyes, when someone recounted them to him, seemed to unfold from another point of view, as if he were standing on the top of one of those mountains in Ikons, and could see the stones as the apostles on the mountains saw them, and not as the faithful observer did from below.

Now, this is where Bakhtin's ideas become really slippery, because, as Vice (1997) reports, the mixing of intentions between speaker and listener means that dialogism is not analysable, and the *actual meaning* is constituted solely within the voices of the dialogic interaction. In other words, the use of well-worn words, although used in the same or similar order, can have differing actual meaning depending on the dialogic interaction. This is fundamental to the analytical approach I am undertaking, because it is not an approach that seeks to find truth, but an approach that seeks to *uncover* through exploring *conjecture*. Like Bakhtin, I could make no claim to actual meaning, only that symbolic meaning exists in the images presented.

Drawing together metaphor, symbolism and dialogic

I have come to suggest that there is something comparable between the process of dialogism and the generation of an image in that it supports a consciousness-raising experience between oneself and others. This, however, is not the way that Bakhtin (1981) appears to see the application of conscious imagery, for his focus is clearly that of a science of language, linguistics and literature. Paul de Man (2003) notes that Bakhtin made some very clear delineation between what he considered dialogism and discourses found within poetry and prose. This separating of multi-voicedness from multi-signedness (i.e. poetry is semiotic, whilst dialogism is voiced) is illustrated in de Man's (2003: 345) citing of Bakhtin (1981) on this subject:

> [No] matter how one understands the interrelationship of meanings in a poetic symbol (or trope) this relationship is never of the dialogical sort; it is impossible under any conditions or at any time to imagine

a trope (say a metaphor) being unfolded into the two exchanges of a dialogue, that is two meanings parcelled out between two separate voices.

How does Bakhtin come to this conclusion? De Man (2003) suggests that, for Bakhtin, the trope is an intentional structure directed towards an object and as such is a pure episteme and not a fact in language (an example of this might be 'sail ahoy', for the sail is not on the sea in isolation but attached to a boat). From a social science perspective, Bakhtin appears here to be positivist in how language can be classified. Poetic and prosaic tropes are therefore excluded from literary discourse and are placed within the field of epistemology in the way in which scientists aim to minimalise independent and dependent variables in their experiments. In essence, de Man argues that Bakhtin's dogma on the nature of dialogism forces a situation whereby as dialogical refraction develops, he is forced to contain the frame and nature of the dialogic experience to the point where there is no room for others of any shape or degree. Polyphony within dialogue, it would appear, is legitimate, whilst polysemy within poetic voice is not (McIntosh, 2008, 2009). The question for me, then, is whether 'poetic symbols' (to use Bakhtin's term, in which I include visual and literary images) can be utilised as a dialogic principle. In order to do this, I would like to present two further images for consideration (see Figures 8 and 9).

In this work, then, perhaps there is an unfolding of the relationship between the author of the images as a parent and as a worker, and the responses they make to being in the situation. What is revealed is an ontological conflict between these two phenomena. The images provide us with a concrete example of an inner landscape turned outwards, a risk in the process of discovery to the image maker, a dynamic of unfolding conflict as it emerges out of the unconscious. It also provides a means for us to sit on the student's shoulder – on the boundary of the threshold – alongside the student, for in the moment it was placed in our relational space it became alive, actually lived, real. It opens up language, it pauses language, and it creates new language. It is a concrete form of abstract themes, and to paraphrase Bakhtin (1984), its essence lies in the tension-filled encounter, on the boundary between the student's consciousness and our own. Through this piece we are able to examine the issues intersubjectively. It is polyphonic as a text, for it plays out different voices; the immediate voices of worker and parent, and within this a multitude of other voices through our own interplay with it. And yet the product is harmonious – a dialogic that offers us the possibility of differing perspectives and commitments within social and ethical life. It is a dialogic

Figure 8 Student B

of the social context, and an explicitly unique example, but we connect with it and understand the relationships that are made within the voices in both their humanistic and systemic discourses. In essence we read both its languaged and non-languaged variables and co-create its plurality within our consciousness. Multi-voicedness emerges from the creation of the visual or literary image itself, and from our encounter at the threshold with the other.

I do not believe that there can be static or rigid interpretations, and I have deliberately avoided a system which enables a precise analysis, because any analysis would not be precise, only a version seen through the lens of my own experiences. Perhaps we also cannot rule out serendipity in this process, for sometimes we are just fortunate with what we find simply by placing things together as we test them. Bakhtin's approach, from a linguistic perspective, would involve a positivist element to this analytical process, and because written text is minimal in the images shown previously, a dialogic in Bakhtin's sense of dialogic is not achievable. However, I feel the principles of Bakhtin's ideas can lead us to an appreciation of the polyphonic qualities that exist within them, and which can further be shared through a field of polyphonic consciousness with

MY WORKING DAY.

The colours reflect my day:
First thing in the morning there is peace
and calm (white)

As the morning progresses, the nausea
intensifies as my son becomes more anxious
(green)

The blackness starts as we leave home +
the anxiety takes hold.

The black continues during the working
day, with a few bright spots as the
day draws to a close.

The yellow is blissful, reunited.

The pink is fun + laughter.

Then the black starts again at
bedtime as he fears he won't live to
see the morning.

Figure 9 Student B

others. This is perhaps a good place to depart from if we choose this type of data upon which to explore a reflective, or indeed reflexive, analysis.

Figures 8 and 9 are two elements of one phenomenon. If we look first at the image (Figure 8), it could be a landscape at dusk or a flag. The author of the image moves to the 'writing on' from the image itself. We are guided through the image by a piece of prose – 'My Working Day' (Figure 9) – which is not about the working day in its traditional sense, because it appears as a labour of everything but being 'at work'. Colours are reflections and metaphors themselves; the blackness is interspersed in the late afternoon with stars that evolve into yellows and pinks. So within this metaphor are other metaphors. The colours are cyclical, and the 'flag' provides us with a statement that suggests 'my working day is not about my day at work, it is about what I think about, and how I feel during my working day'. How many of us can say that our working day consists of thoughts only to do with work? These two forms of text explore the nature of impact of our lives upon our work, and in this case the colours are intertwined with the words to create meaning and understanding:

- White – Calmness
- Green – Nausea
- Black – Anxiety
- Yellow – Bliss
- Pink – Fun, Laughter
- Black – Fear

These are the works of a labour of love. The true working day appears not in the workplace at all; it is at home, in the walk to school, in the reassurance at breakfast, in the storytelling and laughter at bedtime, and in the management of the writer's own feelings that permeate and transcend across all aspects of being. These are not texts of work; they are texts of parenthood. The flag is a unique representation of being a parent, and perhaps more specifically of being a mother, and further to this is the evidence of conflict between this as emotional labour and the labour of employment.

In these pieces there is a searching for a place of safety while writing. In becoming an image-maker and a writer, the author has created a 'zone' in which it is safe to write about the personal. Once this buffer is realised to exist, it opens the doors to other writing. The image and the narrative explored and developed in this work force us to relate to it. They are both *inter*personal and *intra*personal, engaging us in a dynamic of movement, feeling and cognition. Seemingly unconnected at times, on closer inspection they are layered with links to and from one another. The imagery (Figure 8) forms language, communication and text, while the text as language (Figure 9) forms imagery. But we must remember that these are by no means fixed in stone, for, as Sartre (1996) notes, the reflected on is altered profoundly by the reflection because it is self-conscious. The images, then, and that which they represent are fleeting 'once-occurrent events of Being' (Shotter and Billig, 2003: 322). The metaphor becomes a conceptual tool through which the data can be explored.

Forceville (2008), in a discussion of multimodal representations and pictures as metaphor, feels that if metaphors are essential to thinking, then they should not be confined to language, but also occur in music, static and moving images, sounds, gestures, smell and touch – and in permutations of all of these. He sees conceptual metaphor theorists' ignorance of non-verbal metaphor as problematic because it is biased towards a single means of expression – that of language (of which Mercier's (2009) fictional character Amadeus Prado at the beginning of this chapter is so critical). Although much of Forceville's work (1998) has been devoted to pictorial metaphor, in this instance a multimodal approach is more appropriate. Forceville (2008: 463) suggests multimodal metaphors as metaphors 'in which target, source ['target' and 'source' are exchanged for 'primary' and 'secondary' subjects in Black's work], and/or mappable features are represented or suggested by at least two different sign systems (one of whom may be language) or modes of perception'. He outlines four major factors which he feels play a role: first, these metaphors are apprehended differently to verbal counterparts, having an immediacy not captured in language; second, they cue the similarity between the target and the source of the metaphor differently from language; third, as music or pictures, they have more cross-cultural access than verbal metaphors; finally, they have a stronger emotional appeal than verbal metaphors.

On the work of John Kennedy (1982), Forceville (1998: 55–6) notes some primary issues that have bearing on the interpretation of pictorial metaphors, such as those presented above. Among these are:

1 The importance of the viewer in being able to sift out the relevant from the irrelevant in a picture, and determine the governing principles of it rather than accept all features equally. The question of relevance and irrelevance is, for Forceville, linked entirely to what is intended to be conveyed in the image. It is only when this is established that the matter of what is relevant and what is not can be distilled.

2   How are the primary and secondary subjects in pictorial metaphor identified, and on what grounds is this distribution between the two made? (Forceville also notes that this distribution cannot be even, and therefore no reversal of the distribution can be made.)

3   The influence of various contexts in the way in which pictures can be interpreted – for example, the effects of cultural background or genderised experiences may have a bearing on interpretation.

So the identifying of metaphorical devices that exist in the realm of the images themselves is a first step in understanding the way in which abstract information communicated visually can be represented and interpreted – the intentional character understood through what Johns (1984, cited in Forceville, 1998) describes as 'visual literacy'.

As an example, I have constructed a table as a means of developing a form of 'visual literacy' which is based upon the theories discussed in this chapter and in Chapter 3.

Table 1

A coding through the unconscious	A coding through metaphor
• Ideational, as the function of language to communicate tone, ideas and their relationships.	• Extensions of the used part of the metaphor, the use of the novel metaphor and the deepening of metaphorical image constructs through the experience of the speaker and hearer.
• The visibility of the author in their work and their connection to the reader.	
• Ego, persona and the uncovering of self-identification.	• Emphasis, resonance and the interplay of text.
• Production of the unconscious and the decoding and redefining of self.	• Spatial understanding and the context of human beings, and constructs of internal and external landscapes.

An awareness of barriers to self knowing

The shadow and its impact upon psychological growth

The realisation of transformation

• The shifting in self-realisation and the development of individuation.	• The *post-confrontation of self* crisis.

Was Figure 8 ever constructed as a flag? No, it was more an experiment – a 'playing about' with colour on the computer. Suddenly these layers take on new meaning. They begin as the representation of *Being* through colour. White is calm; green, nausea; black, anxiety etc. Then they become a landscape, and perhaps to extend the blackness a little further the addition of stars – yellow-gold beacons in the night – is a fitting contribution to the picture. Perhaps the inspiration for this picture comes not from colour, but from nature. In the way that night turns to day, so white turns to green and so on, returning to white and the cycle is repeated. Without the accompanying prose of Figure 9 we would see it differently – uniquely – to how it is seen through the eyes of its creator, or would be unable to connect with the experience they illustrate. Indeed, our own 'reading' of these texts will resonate with us personally in different ways. Pierre Bayard (2008) notes that even when we have read the same books, when discussing them we may feel we have read something entirely different, and it is the same with images and any prose. Perhaps the representation in Figure 8 is a type of 'badge' or blanket. The writer wraps herself up in it, because she is inside it, living it. The colours enfold her. At times the flag may lie limp, airless, as she describes in her prose when the blackness takes hold; at other times it may flap wildly in the breeze, the yellows and pinks invigorating, the stars moments of bliss as the end of the working day draws near.

There is no doubt that the imagery laid out in Figures 8 and 9 communicates a set of ideations and the relationships between them in the way that Forceville's (2008) factors suggest they can. The 'flag' is functional. It sets a tone and uses devices that are familiar and associative through its use of colour and shapes. We can connect with it through these familiar associations, and from it a movement of feeling occurs. It is not language but it communicates, and creates a 'sense' in the way that Riceour (2003) describes – it is not named (by word) but we know it by our experiences of feeling and contiguity. Meaning-making is then derived from it. Figure 9 supplies this through the writer's own hand, and then it is laid out before the viewer/reader who imposes their own meaning, and so a new text emerges.

Furthermore, where is it that we find emphasis and resonance within this work? First, where does it sit within a literal system? And, second, what is our degree of response to it – the way we interpret it and its implicative elaboration? For the former, we can return to the title of the piece – 'My Working Day' – and the original realisation that this is not a literal representation of work, more one of emotional labour. Both of the images engage us in multiple possibilities, the variations of meaning within the literal context of the working day. For the latter, we engage emotionally in our interpretation, and from it we are able once again to 'sense' the complexity of what is as much unsaid as said. This is the essence of its implicative elaboration.

Conclusion

If a tension exists between the usage of metaphor and dialogics as separate forms of communication, then perhaps when interpreting visual and literary images we need to be making some choices about our approach. Is our approach one of examining pictorial and multimodal metaphor through Forceville's (2008) ideas or one of examining the dialogic in a Bakhtinian sense? In other words are we searching for what is symbolic through visual and literary metaphor, or what is intersubjective in relation to its social action? This is where a tension arises, for as social scientists or reflective practitioners we are not viewing these as purely scholarly disciplines; we are searching for application to the ontological world. The confusion arises when in engaging in the work we not only 'sense' the metaphor but hear the voices and apply new voices, for that is what we have been socialised into doing as researchers and as reflectors on our practices. In effect I believe it goes beyond scholarly activity, such as the study of metaphor or dialogic, and into an applied format. The challenge is in sifting out from the data what is metaphor and what is voice, for it is all too easy for them to become conflated into some strange hybrid of a linguistic and symbolic origin.

   Finally, the images that have been presented so far, and the way we can work upon them, suggest that we can approach them unidimensionally, either as metaphors or as a dialogic, but we can also approach them interdimensionally by utilising both of these approaches alongside one another – a kind of mixed methodology if you please, with the prospect of deepening understanding and developing theory through conjectures of what is found. What is perhaps most important is that in doing so we establish the differing methods from the outset, and once this is done we can either define them as separate constructs found within the data or build upon them accordingly, using what is found to shape new constructs from them. In order to conduct this effectively, we need to create models from these concepts which provide us with a systematic foundation and allow us to follow patterns in the images themselves, rather than just viewing them in the hope that something will emerge. Furthermore, as Forceville (1998: 41) points out,

[A]n important consequence of the fact that the referant is created by the very act of producing the metaphor is that no truth/falsehood test can be applied. But the fact that creative metaphor is not amenable to a truth/falsehood judgment does not entail that it has no cognitive import. Since it is possible to pronounce on a creative metaphor's appropriateness or aptness, a creative metaphor can contribute something to our understanding and perceptions of the world.

If we can use these approaches to build models for research and reflection able to stand the test of rigour, then I believe there is infinite potential for uncovering crucial new aspects of professional practice.

References

Adler, G., Fordham, M. and Read, H. (eds) (1953–78) *The Collected Works of C.G. Jung*. Routledge. London

Bachelard, G. (1994) *The Poetics of Space*. Beacon Press. Boston

Bakhtin, M. (1981) *Dialogical Imagination*. (Trans. Holquist, M.) University of Texas Press. Austin

Bakhtin, M. (1984) *Problems of Dostoevsky's Poetics*. University of Minnesota Press. Minneapolis

Bayard, P. (2008) *How to Talk about Books You Haven't Read*. Granta Books. London

Black, M. (1998) More about Metaphor. In Ortony, A., *Metaphor and Thought* (2nd edn). Cambridge University Press. Cambridge

Bohm, D. (2004) *On Creativity*. Routledge. London

Carter, R. (2007) *Language and Creativity: The Art of Common Talk*. Routledge. London

Culler, J. (1982) *Saussure*. Fontana. London

De Man, P. (2003) Dialogue and Dialogism. In Gardiner, M., *Mikhail Bakhtin*, Vol 3. Sage. London

Derrida, J. (1976) *Of Grammatology*. Johns Hopkins University Press. Baltimore

Derrida, J. (1981) *Positions*. Athlone Press. London

Derrida, J. (1988) *Limited Inc*. North Western University Press. Evanston

Eco, U. (2003) *Baudolino*. Vintage. London

Edgar, I. (2004) *Guide to Imagework: Imagination Based Research Methods*. Routledge. London

Fainsilber, L. and Ortony, A. (1987) Metaphorical Use of Language in the Study of Emotion. *Metaphor in Symbolic Activity*. 2: 239–50

Forceville, C. (1998) *Pictorial Metaphor in Advertising*. Routledge. London

Forceville, C. (2008) Metaphor in Pictures and Multimodal Representations. In

Gibbs, R.W., *The Cambridge Handbook of Metaphor and Thought*. Cambridge University Press. Cambridge

Foucault, M. (2002) *Interview with Michel Foucault*. In Faubion, J.D., *Power: Essential Works of Foucault 1954–1984*. Penguin. London

Gibbs, R.W. (1999) *The Poetics of Mind*. Cambridge University Press. Cambridge.

Gibbs, R.W. (ed.) (2008) *The Cambridge Handbook of Metaphor and Thought*. Cambridge University Press. Cambridge

Glendinning, S. (1998) *On Being with Others: Heidegger, Derrida, Wittgenstein*. Routledge. London

Gurevitch, Z. (2003) Plurality in Dialogue. In Gardiner, M., *Mikhail Bakhtin*, Vol 3. Sage. London

James, W. (1982) *The Varieties of Religious Experience*. Penguin Classics. London

Johns, B. (1984) Visual Metaphor: Lost and Found. *Semiotica*. 52(3/4): 291–333

Jung, C. (2005) *The Archetypes and the Collective Unconscious* (2nd edn). Routledge. London

Kennedy, J.M. (1982) Metaphor in Pictures. *Perception*. 11: 589–605

Kittay, E.F. (1987) *Metaphor: Its Cognitive Force and Linguistic Structure*. Clarendon Press. Oxford

Lakoff, G. (1990) The Invarience Hypothesis: Is Abstract Reason Based on Image-Schemas? *Cognitive Linguistics*. 1: 39–74

Lakoff, G. and Johnson, M. (2003) *Metaphors We Live by*. University of Chicago Press. Chicago and London

McIntosh, P. (2008) Reflective Reproduction: A Figurative Approach to Reflecting in, on, and about Action. *Educational Action Research*. 16(1): 125–43

McIntosh, P. (2009) The Puzzle of Metaphor and Voice in Arts-Based Social Research. *International Journal of Social Research Methodology*. 99999: 1. Published through iFirst, 09/06/09: http://dx.doi.org/10.1080/136455 70902969357

McMullen, L.M. (2008) Putting It in Context: Metaphor and Psychotherapy. In Gibbs, R.W., *The Cambridge Handbook of Metaphor and Thought*. Cambridge University Press. Cambridge

Mercier, P. (2009) *Night Train to Lisbon*. Atlantic Books. London

Nealon, J.T. (2003) The Ethics of Dialogue: Bakhtin and Levinas. In Gardiner, M., *Mikhail Bakhtin*, Vol 4. Sage. London

Ortony, A. (1998) *Metaphor and Thought* (2nd edn). Cambridge University Press. Cambridge

Ricoeur, P. (2003) *The Rule of Metaphor: The Creation of Meaning in Language*. Routledge. London

Salman, S. (1999) The Creative Psyche: Jung's Major Contributions. In Young-Eisendrath, P. and Dawson, T., *The Cambridge Companion to Jung*. Cambridge University Press. Cambridge

Sartre, J.P. (1996) *Being and Nothingness*. Routledge. London

Shotter, J. and Billig, M. (2003) A Bakhtinian Psychology: From Out of the Heads of Individuals and Into the Dialogues between Them. In Gardiner, M., *Mikhail Bakhtin*, Vol 4. Sage. London

Talbot, M. (1995) *Fictions at Work: Language and Social Practice in Fiction*. Longman. London

Tuan, Y.F. (2003) *Space and Place: The Perspective of Experience*. University of Minnesota Press. Minneapolis

Vice, S. (1997) *Introducing Bakhtin*. Manchester University Press. Manchester

Von Franz, M.L. (1978) The Process of Individuation. In Jung, C., *Man and His Symbols*. Picador. London

Whiston Spirn, A. (1998) *The Language of Landscape*. Yale University Press. London

Chapter 6

Infinite possibilities of knowing and transformation

A new angelology of words is needed so that we may once again have faith in them. Without the inherence of the angel in the word – and angel means originally 'emissary', 'message bearer' – how can we utter anything but personal opinions, things made up in our subjective minds? How can anything of worth and soul be conveyed from one psyche to another, as in a conversation, a letter, a book, if archetypal significances are not carried in the depths of our words?

(Hillman, 1992: 9)

Introduction

In this chapter, I shall attempt to bring together some of the major strands that have featured in the book so far, and discuss them in conjunction with the kinds of imagery and text that have formed the basis for my empirical work in this area. The fundamental aim of this work has been to explore the ways in which 'transformation' – both personal and professional – can be established through ways which are accessible to us all through engaging in the creative process, and in so doing foster cultures of critical creativity within the varying health, social and educational domains of professional practice. This can occur through a number of routes which can be grounded in 'learning', 'human inquiry' or 'research', or as a transcendence of both concepts and practices. Having established a conceptual and theoretical platform in the previous chapters, this can now be explored more fully as a 'practice'.

Methodology and transformation

Two central problems warrant further discussion, and both centre on the concept of transformation, but from different perspectives. First, there is the issue of rigour. To refine this work further, we need a solid methodological approach to its conduct as a method of research or human inquiry. It is not enough, in my view, to say, 'Here is an image or poem. It is open to conjecture and here is my conjecture.' Equally, it is not enough to say, 'Here is my conjecture based on a framework to analyse it.' Why? Because it does not set out a principle in which the work is undertaken, either as a research process or as an approach to learning. First, therefore, we need to apply these ideas from within a methodological context.

Second, we need to locate this methodological context within a more theoretical framework. Michel Foucault, in very broad terms, focused on the concept of transformation. It is therefore useful to ask one of the fundamental Foucauldian questions: 'What made this transformation possible?' In this sense to 'problematise' (to borrow from Foucault) all that has come before as an epistemic break. This chapter therefore concludes with a short discussion on 'rupture'.

I have already discussed action research in Chapter 2, so I do not wish to retread this ground, but rather to add to it. First, I would like to say that this methodology is very much in its infancy. It draws upon a wide range of theories in its development, the strands of which can be interwoven to form a colour and texture. Then, in good action research tradition, they become not an end but a series of beginnings. This means that the process of developing and constructing such an approach to inquiry is not linear, for it veers into areas of theory and practice which have not ordinarily formed part of an action research domain. This is of significance as I move towards a structure and recommendations for use.

Archetypal imagery and critical reflection

The philosophy that underpins my approach can now be clearly identified as that of the practitioner-researcher, as subscribed to by Fish (1998) as an example. This critically reflexive approach can also be seen from within an action research construct as it is fundamentally aimed at a better understanding of both self and practice – a transformative process – and the grasping of the process and its theoretical underpinning are demonstrated in the work produced in the images provided. These images are important both in their own right, as symbolic, meaningful activities, and as possible 'data' in action research methods that I wish to discuss further.

So, to turn then to the application of the archetypal image, Edgar (2004) notes that imagework has existed under a number of guises: 'active imagination', 'visualisation' and 'guided fantasy' are all terms under which the notion of imagework falls; and the basis for such work is Jung's (2005) concept of the collective unconscious. On the subject of imagework from within the qualitative research domain, Edgar (2004) notes the dearth of image-based research methodologies in existence. It is in the field of transpersonal psychology that the use of imagework has emerged more purposefully as a method of research. Edgar cites Anderson (1998: 69), who states:

> [Transpersonal psychology] seeks to delve deeply into the most profound and inexplicable aspects of human experiences, including mystical and unitive experiences, experiences of transformation, extraordinary insight, meditative awareness, altered states of consciousness, and self actualisation.

According to Edgar (2004: 127), this process is 'intuitive inquiry', and within it there is the use of 'various altered states of consciousness, active dreaming and dream incubation, mystical vision and audition, intentional imaging, kinaesthetic and somatic awareness, and states of consciousness more typically associated with the artistic process than with science, in all the phases of inquiry' (Anderson, 1998: 76).

Edgar (2004) feels that experiential methods (imagework being one) can evoke and articulate self-identities and implicit knowledge in ways that other methods cannot. In the context of this work, comparisons can be made with the creation of the images as 'intentional imaging' as the primary element in this 'intuitive inquiry'. Furthermore, Edgar identifies a number of fields within imagework: *introductory imagework, memory imagework* and *spontaneous imagework*. He includes active imagination in the process of spontaneous imagework – 'a spontaneous journey into the imagination' (Edgar, 2004: 128).

Perhaps at this point some clarity is needed with regard to the relationship between 'intentional imaging' and 'spontaneous imagework', as I perceive it. The latter refers to the active use of the imagination and its representation in some visual or textual form. The former refers to the 'specificness' of the image – the placing of symbols within the image itself. Edgar (2004) suggests that the processing of imagework into forms of data generally has up to four stages; first, a descriptive stage where respondents 'tell their story'; second, an analysis of the personal meaning of the experience and of the symbols used; third, an analysis of the models used to inform their imagery; and finally a comparative stage where respondents share and compare their imagework.

To illustrate, we can return to our images and poetry. In addition to the images or pieces of writing themselves, the students were asked to construct a critical commentary on their work – a reflection on the reflective process itself. This aids in addressing the stages designed by Edgar. (For the purposes of my work, I wish to include the first three stages, as the fourth is a quite specific pedagogic stage.)

Stage 1: The descriptive stage

'For I am lost,
not recently Lost,
No, I've been lost for years.
I don't know
when I got mislaid

I think that
I slowly slipped away
I am behind the mirror
I am in the puddle,
hidden in the mud.'

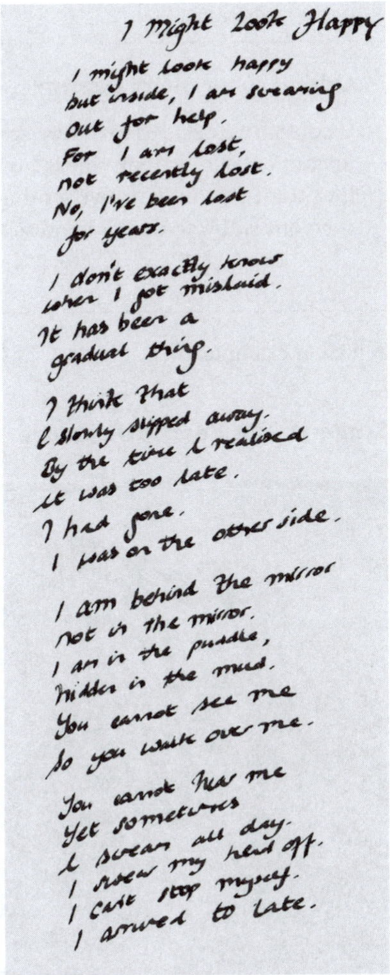

Figure 7 Student C

Stage 2: The personal meaning of the symbols used

Critical commentary excerpt:

'Using a pen and ink made the writing seem natural, raw and rough around the edges; I was making my own mark.'

Stage 3: An analysis of the models used to inform their imagery

> **Critical commentary excerpt:**
>
> 'I could have decided to ignore certain aspects that I felt would be uncomfortable. I think this is how writing transformed at times into third person. Creative writing permits story telling. But not everyone is able to do this because they do not know who they are.'
>
> (John 2002)

A further example:

Stage 1: The descriptive stage

Figure 5 Student A

Stage 2: The personal meaning of the symbols used

Narrative addition to the image:

(Frame 3) represents the memory, the assembly of the Trust Board members, a lucid recollection of people sitting fused by the table between us. I failed to see them as individuals, but a gathering of bodies. The **TABLE** appears as a vast expanse, an obstacle between us. The **MOUNTAINS** represent the enormity of the task ahead, the scale of responsibility I faced. Mountains I was not convinced I could scale. The faces around the table are presented only by **EYES** and **OBJECTS** staring intensely in my direction, no features apparent. I have no other recollection of the individuals just the sternness of their stare. My sole task was to represent facts and data in the most precise manner possible to attain permission and funding to instigate change. Towards the rear of the frame are **QUIET WATERS, SUMMER CLOUDS AND SUN RAYS** (and £ signs) representing the PEACE I began to experience part way through the session as I realized I was making an impact. I became surprisingly **CALM** and **CONFIDENT** as the session progressed, these relaxed feelings were out of character. The seasonal outlook beyond the darkened silhouette are images I associate with **CONTENTMENT, EASE AND PEACEFULNESS** I was experiencing . . . I realized a goal, I could envisage the next stage of the journey which brought with it more settled ground.'

Stage 3: An analysis of the models used to inform their imagery

Critical commentary excerpt:

'When anger or despair dominates reason the Child is in control, at this time my internal reactions to an external event were making it impossible for me to make any rational plan to resolve the issue. I remained within this frame from over 10 years.

At this point, then, there is the development of an image or a series of images. We can see at first glance that they form the basis of a *reflexive critique* – the 'account' is collected, or in this case constructed. These images and prose do not exist in isolation. They are grounded in what the creator understands as the 'fact' of a situation – such as particular patterns of institutional behaviour, perceptions of self, and the consideration of what is normal within these given situations. In doing so, the images are attempting to make implicit authoritative claims to the understanding of these situations, their causes and motivations which 'probably' explain these facts.

Not only do these images put forward these sets of understanding from the perspective of the individual's experiences, either informally from everyday experiences or from those which are more professionally driven, they are located in a place designed to communicate with others – if they can connect with the experiences of others, then these experiences may be considered to be generally true. The 'reflexive capability', as Winter (1989) puts it, is in the ability to question these claims of authority as the factual state of affairs and generality. From this, the 'image' becomes something which is not simply factual or universal law based on a body of knowledge, but a means to open up multiple lines of inquiry – to explore alternative accounts that may be relevant or important. It is what Winter refers to as making the reflexive basis of the account explicit so that further questions can be layered upon it.

At this point I wish to depart from Winter's thinking, for his is an approach of collaboration, and, at present, my thinking on action research is that it can be both collaborative and personal – at least it reaches its potential through a different route. In my work the dialogue (or dialectic, as Winter (1989) terms it) is approached through different means. As with Winter, there is a prising apart of ideologies, and the development of significance in the work, but it is achieved through the utilisation of a 'dialogical landscape' as opposed to a dialectical construction. Significance emerges through internal discussions on phenomena and context. It is at this point that the participants in the inquiry encounter a crisis – the 'threshold', as Bakhtin would suggest.

Folch-Serra (2003) notes that Bakhtin wanted to find connections between all degrees of plurality and otherness (as opposed to Winter, who views plurality as a collage of contradictions). He further suggests that Bakhtin had an awareness of how human beings use language as a means to their agency. Returning to my earlier notion of 'landscape', a landscape in this view can be defined as the geographical conditions in which voices are allowed to express themselves in ways that they would not ordinarily do in other conditions. Referring to dialogism in relation to this, Shotter and Billig (2003: 322) put it eloquently:

> [In other words], dialogical events always give rise to something unique and unrepeatable . . . it is in these only 'once-occurrent events of Being', in these brief and fleeting moments that we not only express ourselves and 'show' each other the nature of our own unique 'inner' lives, but we also shape our living relations both to each other and our surroundings. It is in these unique, dialogical or relational moments also that we can reshape (in some small degree) the already existing historical and ideological influences at work in spontaneously and routinely shaping our ways of relating ourselves to each other and our surroundings.

This is of particular importance if we consider that in effect a dialogic unconsciousness (Shotter and Billig, 2003) is occurring, and that in this dialogic unconsciousness the language used in interaction may be either expressive or repressive. In the process of moving away from the 'literal word' to more figurative approaches to representation, the question of expression and repression shifts to one of interpretation. The dialogic experience is not so much that one speaks or writes repressively, but is about what is seen in the image – whether what one sees or reads appears to contain these qualities. In this case it is that whilst a conscious space exists between parties, the dialogic unconscious in relation to the communication is held equally, but with not necessarily a commonly held perception of the world, for different expressions or repressions may exist within those unique dialogic unconscious experiences.

Some examples of my own experiences of engaging in the images may be of use to explore this, first through a response to Figures 8 and 9:

> These are works of a labour of love. The true working day is not in the workplace at all, it is at home, in the walk to school, in the reassurance at breakfast, in the storytelling and laughter at bedtime, and in the management of her own feelings that permeate and transcend across all aspects of her being. These are not texts of work, they are texts of motherhood. The flag is a unique representation of being a parent, and probably more specifically, of being a mother.
>
> (McIntosh, 2006: 220)

Second, through two additional images:

Tears are funny things, they slip out, unnoticed at first. Then suddenly they are runny all down my face, and I am a mess. My nose is runing, so unattractive. My face is red and blotchy, my lips are stained and swollen. I look absolutely awful. I feel really stupid and embarrassed. People in the office are surprised, and possibly feel awkward. I am more surprised than they are. I did not see this coming at all.

Denial you see, is my middle name.

Figure 10 Student C

ME

I am born, I enter the world,
Dazed and weary.
Relief as I nestle
In my Mother's warmth.

I'm a child, comforted
With a threadbare toy,
I suck my thumb,
My world is my Parents.

I start school, dressed
Smartly in my uniform
I conform to the rules
Yet I enjoy it all.

Secondary school begins
My confidence that was
Begins to fail me,
I do no longer like school.

Figure 11 Student C

Sixth form College,
With relief I part from
School, Freedom calls,
I start to find myself.

I am a student nurse
I have found myself
Wonderful place,
Loyal friends.

I am a Sister,
Responsibility looms
Kind and fair
I'd like to think.

I am a Lecturer
I am struggling
I am fighting
I am surviving.

Figure 11   continued

'Denial you see, is my middle name.'

This aspect of herself she even includes as part of her name, because it is to her an integral part of the ego – there, in the centre of her consciousness. There is also the juxtaposition between components of the poem 'Me' [Figure 11] and the piece 'Tears' [Figure 10]. In 'Tears' we are engaged in her confrontation with the sudden cry from nowhere, which we can understand as her own sudden acknowledgement of things denied. In 'Me' we see the post-response to denial, the confrontation with what has been denied. 'I am struggling, I am fighting, I am surviving.'

(McIntosh, 2006: 265)

The expression of our inner worlds in such surroundings through this process not only reshapes our own existing relationships to ourselves, but contributes to the reshaping of others through their exposure to it, and this is where Winter's (1989) dialectic emerges in terms of questions and propositions if these dialogues are considered as data. The data illustrated throughout here is essentially self-generated and self-generating, for it sets up an individual propositional framework for inquiry, both for the composer of the work and for the viewer/reader of it. From the participant's point of view, in order to come to this point a series of phases are worked through, which are inclusive of active imagination. Remember Hannah's (2001: 7) statement: '[T]he further we go, the more we realize that every widening of consciousness is indeed the greatest gain we can make'? Student B illustrates this as a continuum of her experience:

'I have collected pictures + words expressing how stupid this assignment is. I don't want to do it and I don't think I can do it.' (Diary extract from portfolio)

Figure 8 Student B

MY WORKING DAY.

The colours reflect my day:
First thing in the morning there is peace
and calm (white)
As the morning progresses, the nausea
intensifies as my son becomes more anxious
             (green)
The blackness starts as we leave home +
the anxiety takes hold.
The black continues during the working
day, with a few bright spots as the
day draws to a close.
The yellow is blissful, reunited.
The pink is fun + laughter.
Then the black starts again at
bedtime as he fears he won't live to
See the morning.

Figure 9 Student B

Critical commentary excerpt:

'The colour chart helped me to look at myself objectively and reach
a better understanding. Using artwork helps you to 'feel' the
situation and can be more expressive than words'.

What is it, then, that separates out active imagination as having potential as a methodological tool, as opposed to, for instance, dream analysis? Hannah (2001) suggests it is more empirical and scientific in character, and as a method has a long tradition in 'man' (her term) as a dialogue between eternal powers and the coming to terms with them. In Jung's therapeutic terms, this suggests the uncovering of opposites that live within the unconscious and uniting them with ourselves. Salman (1999: 55) notes that Jung conceived the relationship between the ego and the remainder of the psyche to be one of a continuous dialogue; a never-ending process within which the nature of the conversation is one of constant change. It is perhaps in the use of creative and symbolic unconscious material that these phenomena can be captured more clearly.

Salman (1999) suggests that symbols emerge from the unconscious, and are not censored or distorted; nor are they signs for something else. They are, as Salman (1999: 65) puts it,

> like living things, pregnant with meaning and capable of acting like transformers of psychic energy . . . Symbolic images are genuine transformers of psychic energy because a symbolic image evokes the totality of the archetype it reflects. Images evoke the aim and motivation of instincts through the psychoid nature of the archetype.

Jung harnessed the symbolic images through active imagination processes, such as painting and drawing, and, as Salman (1999) describes it, once these expressions are 'in the bottle' a dialogue can be much more easily entered into. Below are some images captured 'in the bottle'.

As we can see, these images serve very different purposes: the first requires an accompanying narrative to illuminate and explicate; the second is a more direct message to the reader. The motivations are unique, the psychic energy evident in both.

Salman (1999) also notes that Jung considered that there were two types of thinking – rational and non-rational – and within these constructs two different modes of processing of information take place. There is an imagistic, symbolising component to the mind which works by analogy and correspondence as opposed to rational explanation. Salman suggests that Jung's belief was that this type of thought was an indicator that it is pre-determined to its archetypal origins – those patterns of behaviour and the unconscious that constitute the contingencies between man's history and the present. Drawing on mythological motifs and interpreting them in the light of modern dreams and fantasies, Jung developed the method of 'archetypal amplification'. In this method the symbol is taken to have a meaning grounded in the historicity and what is known about that

Figure 1 Student A

Figure 2 Student B

symbol – so, for instance, Salman (1999) uses the symbol of the river to connect with constructs of immersion, purification and dissolution. In mythology the river has an identity as a healer and as a sacred entity. What occurs, then, is that the psyche selects a particular image from its catalogue of images available from the experience of the individual in order to serve a quite specific metaphorical purpose.

This can be seen to some degree in Figures 1 and 2, for both, entirely independently, have employed Munch's *The Scream*. This image is so iconic that its deployment can be used as a most symbolic communication. It exists not only in the 'image catalogue' of the writer, but in the image catalogue of the viewer/reader. There is no doubt on the part of either party as to its metaphorical purpose. Below is another example of both an archetype and a metaphor:

Shadow

I walk the short distance to college. The sun is beating down on me, and I enjoy feeling the warmth through my clothes. It seems so unfair that I must go indoors. Suddenly something black darts around me. "Hey!" I shout "Watch out, you could have knocked me flying. Yet when I look around me, I can see no-one. Then again, a shadow dashes around me. It's my shadow; it's not supposed to do that.

"Come with me!" it says, teasingly. "Why would you want to be indoors on a day like this?" Is this really happening? I look all around me once again. Thankfully no-one is there, except a shadow, my shadow tapping its foot menacingly. I look at my own feet; they are firmly planted on the ground.

"Well make your mind up. Why are you always so indecisive? Let's go, we can escape from here and have fun, not like this college lark. There is so much more to see, so much more to be!"

I look up at the college façade: bricks, windows, scaffolding; hardly enticing. But I take a deep sigh. I can't escape today. I grab the shadow, my shadow, and shove it in my bag quickly, before it is seen. How did it work loose again? The trouble it could have caused me. I will stitch it back on when I get home. I brace myself, put my shoulders back, and hold up my chin. I can do this, and I climb the college steps. I go inside to face another day.

Figure 12 Student C

In earlier work, Student A talks of 'quiet waters, summer clouds and sun rays', while in 'Shadow' Student C writes, 'The sun is beating down on me, and I enjoy feeling the warmth through my clothes'. Even though neither perhaps has much knowledge of myths of the sun or water, they form part of the imagery, and are employed as metaphors of reassurance, warmth, comfort, revitalisation and recuperation. They restore or soothe, depending on the nature of the context.

Also of note in 'Shadow' is the way in which the shadow is portrayed both as a dark character and as a trickster. It not only tries to persuade a diversion from that which is necessary but unwanted, but does so as if it is a high-spirited child seeking space to be free.

Within imaginal psychology, the method encourages the individual into the proliferation of evocative images which enable descriptive qualities and implicit metaphors in adherence with particular phenomena. The images themselves above, and the qualitative descriptions of them, therefore allow for elaborate metaphorical implications to be placed upon them. Student A provides us with the elaborate metaphorical images in, for instance, Figures 1, 4, 5 and 6, and then supplies a telling statement within her critical commentary which adds substantially to their qualitative description:

Critical commentary:

Commencing this I assumed that my whole learning experience would be centred around the trust board presentation (Figure 5) and my feeling before and after. I was wrong, the majority of self analysis has come from the first frame (Figure 1) that spanned a decade. This frame interestingly was a late addition to the imagery as my prime concern had always been centred around the audit presentation, in reality only totalling 20 minutes of my existence. I am now travelling through what would be stage 5 as I address the fear of freedom.'

Vannoy Adams (1999) takes a very brief look at the nature of the analysis of an image. In this he identifies two conflicting approaches to the purpose of this process. First, he suggests that, for Jung, the function of the unconscious is to construct compensatory perspectives to the biases that may be held by the conscious, such as partial or defective attitudes. The aim of this process is ultimately the individuation of the ego in relation to the self. What is repressed, ignored or neglected by the conscious is compensated for by the unconscious, and it is the opportunity that this provides to the integration of the psyche that is sought. The poems by Student C (Figures 11 and 12) are wonderful examples of this kind of compensatory process made real. Arguably, this form of archetypal psychology has its roots more firmly planted in phenomenology than in other more positivist analyses, and Figures 11 and 12 are both rich in phenomenological 'soul' or psyche. What is also evident in these pieces is the way in which the ego, persona and shadow are seen to operate actively in ways which compensate and equalise within the psyche. The 'freeing up' of the ego so that it is able to allow in the 'other' is the crucial factor methodologically in the application of this process, and the three students' work bears witness to this achievement.

In the work so far, then, there are some theoretical ideas as to how the process of coming to know oneself takes place, but in themselves they cannot necessarily be described as systematic, but rather as imaginal descriptors. Chodorow (1997) takes Jung's ideas of active imagination and provides a structure in which they can operate from a more functional perspective. First, as part of the grounding of this structure, I want to introduce a term that underpins it: *betrachten*.

Chodorow (1997: 7), in a discussion of the starting points for active fantasy, notes: 'In German there is a word "betrachten" that means making something pregnant by giving it your attention. This special way of looking is reminiscent of a child's experience when absorbed in symbolic play.' Previous to this, she cites Jung (1932: 3) on the significance of such a term in his ideas:

> Looking, psychologically, brings about the activation of the object: it is as if something were emanating from one's spiritual eye that evokes or activates the object of one's vision.
>
> The English verb 'to look at' does not convey this meaning, but the German 'betrachten', which is an equivalent, means also to make pregnant . . . And if it is pregnant, then something is due to come out of it; it is alive, it produces, it multiplies. That is the case with the fantasy image: one concentrates upon it, and then one has great difficulty in keeping the thing quiet, it gets restless, it shifts, something is added, or it multiplies itself; one fills it with living power and it becomes pregnant.

So what bearing does *betrachten* have on a systematic approach to active imagination? Chodorow (1997) suggests that active imagination has two parts or stages: first, letting the unconscious come up; and second, coming to terms with that unconscious. In a discussion of the first step, Jung feels that this involves the suspension of our rational and critical faculties so that fantasy can be freed – to 'let things happen'. The task in this process is to gain access to our unconscious contents, and it is the unconscious which takes the lead while the ego serves as a kind of attentive witness or note-keeper. It is in this way of looking that Jung sees the potential for *betrachten* – a way of looking that brings things alive.

I believe two forms of looking occur in the approach I am advocating. First, that which occurs in the active imagination process; and second, subjecting the works to a metaphorical analysis. Although the initial images are given life in their original commentaries states, a second life is borne out of the application of metaphorical analysis to them.

In the second part of active imagination it is consciousness which takes the lead. As the images of the unconscious flow into awareness, the ego begins to participate in the experience. It is in this part that a string of insights may occur, which require evaluation and integration, and these will undoubtedly involve questions of meaning and moral demand. Chodorow (1997: 10) writes that 'All the parts of an issue are laid out so that differences can be seen and resolved.' As was noted in Chapter 3, it is a question of balance between aesthetics and science that allows for a reflective analytic.

How these two facets come together can be seen in the work of Student B. At first there is a stifling of 'letting things happen', a disallowance of the irrational and incomprehensible to become 'real'.

Portfolio diary extract:

'This module is so stupid. I feel so bloody cross that I have got to do this. I just don't think I can – I don't understand it + I know that I can't write poetry or draw'.

Then comes the production of an image (Figure 2) where she recognises that an image of this exists in some form of reality just as other material objects exist. As these images become 'archetypal' they become concrete entities upon which abstract themes can be developed.

Finally, there is a commentary on the experience:

Critical commentary:

'The process became effective when I reflected on the artwork and my feelings. The initial collage (Figure 2) provided a means of expression which facilitated reflection. The process of writing during the reflection process was empowering and involved free-flowing writing, diary entries and letter writing'.

By 'letting things happen' a collage emerges as a concrete entity upon which the abstract themes within the reflection were enabled to take place and facilitate other forms of image.

A return to a dialogic ethic

Until this point the notion of dialogics has not been discussed as an ethic – morally or methodologically. I have referred to it conceptually, to a degree, and as a means of exploring forms of interaction, but if one is to suggest that dialogics has value from a methodological perspective, then one needs to consider it as a form of ethical practice. Nealon (2003) refers to the work of Horkheimer and Adorno (1972) on the idea of the enlightenment subject. In this notion, the enlightenment subject seeks to escape from static forms of knowing, such as those built on nature and myth, through knowledge-gathering adventures and experiences. The 'instrumental' subject actively confronts 'otherness' through seeking out hazards and engaging in risk. Using classical mythology to describe this, Horkheimer and Adorno suggest that Odysseus (a wanderer) has to lose himself before he is able to find himself. On this basis, Nealon (2003) suggests that in order to find oneself, one must return not inwardly to the unity found within the *cogito*, but outwardly to the diversity and risk of the other so that one may lose oneself in order that an adventure of appropriation occurs that can confront and conquer these never-ending forms of otherness. In doing so, one is able to make use of the other, and find oneself by means of the other. The other effectively becomes a mirror upon which we are able to see ourselves at new and deeper levels. It is within this system that an ethical framework begins to emerge which is inclusive of the subjects of dialogics and metaphor.

What emerges out of this are two distinct constructs: first, a dialogic intersubjectivity understood as an impassioned play of voices; and second, voice as a metaphor that best accommodates conflicting desires. The dialogic as multi-voicedness is therefore a powerful metaphor in itself within which other forms of otherness can be considered from non-threatening positions, and through which voices and responses can occur. Nealon (2003) cites the work of Baumann (1993: 84) in suggesting 'A Postmodern ethics would be one that readmits the Other as a neighbor . . . an ethics that recasts the Other as the crucial character in the process through which the moral self comes into its own.' In this sense, then, the ethic comes from what Nealon (2003: 140) describes as 'an open and ongoing obligation to respond to the other, rather than a static march to some philosophical end or conclusion'.

In my own notes on the analysis of the data illustrated in the figures above, I write:

> We may not have experienced these exact emotions in the way that
> the writer does, or the experiences themselves, because they are

unique to them. But we know as human beings how we feel these things individually. The writer is reliant on the reader to make interpretations as the 'being in' of these experiences, otherwise they become surreal, unconnected elements that are visually and experientially of little resonance. Our own experiences enable us to extend the metaphors within our own places of experience. There may be commonalities, but these commonalities are experienced uniquely, as Jung (2005) suggests.

(McIntosh, 2006: 227)

The reader, therefore, as the Other, has an ethical responsibility to explore the voices and their intersubjective nature, and what we begin to see emerging is a different form of philosophy or ethic. It does not place a phenomenon within certain parameters which would place limitations on the exploration of that or any other connected phenomena, but rather suggests that there is a plurality – a latent plurality within consciousness which can flourish within the 'dialogic'. For Bakhtin, this plurality within dialogics appears to be attacked from the sociological perspective – the dialogic serves as a metaphor upon which the intersubjectivity of a society can be viewed and explored. However, the notion of selfhood and the way it both informs and is informed by the Other is not excluded from the concept. Nealon (2003) discusses this by suggesting that the dialogic offers the opportunity to understand differences and ethical commitments without the requirement to fall upon a universalising or norm-giving structure in the way that other ontological schemes might be constructed. The ethical dialogic then becomes one of social contexts rather than one of ethical rules. As Nealon (2003: 141) suggests, 'they open up a productive horizon to rethink the social landscape of self and other in our groundless postmodern landscape'.

The suggestion, therefore, is that the terms of engagement in this process are found within the dialogics themselves. It is not until we are in them that the 'ground' – the ethical context – begins to emerge, and as a result this ground is not universal, but unique. As Hadjukowski-Ahmed (2003: 355) suggests, 'Dialogism, which is neither dialogue nor dialectics, is a philosophy of communication that maps the discursive territory of difference.' However, I use this term with caution, for whilst I agree with the term 'mapping of discursive territory', I remain unconvinced by the term 'difference', for I believe Hadjukowski-Ahmed is substituting the term 'difference' for the term 'other'. Hadjukowski-Ahmed's work is in relation to participatory action research, and I believe that the term 'difference' should be used explicitly in this context because it relates to a particular form of methodology and the kinds of questions to be asked. Participatory action research as a process is entirely unlike the dialogic inquiry constructed by Bakhtin. So what constitutes 'difference' in these two approaches cannot be the same. In this case this is not necessarily the same as the 'other', which I believe is not in relation to difference, but rather in relation to something which is not yet within our grasp of consciousness. It is not 'different'; it is just 'not yet there'. I believe that creating a discursive territory (dialogism) makes something appear within a space of consciousness so that it may be appropriated, and this can occur at both an internal, individual level and at a level that is socially orientated. My feeling is that Bakhtin may well disagree, for he may feel that this individualistic appropriation is too close to phenomenology, and therefore an individual rather than social approach which is further confined within a set of methodological and philosophical rules, but I believe that methodologically there is scope for duality of purpose as part of the ethical (as a practice rather than a moral construct) application of this mode of inquiry.

Below is an example of a discursive territory of otherness, from which we can see a dialogic with the 'social other' beginning to emerge:

I am lonely
In the class of eighty students
I am afraid
of the students

I am exposed
To a class of eighty students
I am naked
to the students.

I am misunderstood
By a class of eighty students
I hate this
as do the students.

Figure 13 Student C

So, in order to find oneself, one must first become lost, as Horkheimer and Adorno (1972) suggest, and it is in this getting lost that one engages in an unfamiliar world, a world which becomes familiar, and upon which we are able to construct a map or a discursive territory. It is in this discursive territory and through the multiple voices encountered that a new self is found. What is suggested here is that we are both always lost and always found, for we are always within the discursive territory of the other; it is merely the landscape that shifts and changes beneath our feet. Once we understand that the discursive territory acts as a platform to engage us more actively in the dialogic process we can begin to think about the constructs in which this can become realised. Furthermore, Shotter and Billig (1998) look at the nature of cognitive processes such as memory, the languaged claims attached to memory, the strategic roles attached to those memory claims, and the rhetorical functions served within their varying formulations. They discuss that memory appears to be a social rather than an individual action, and that the action of 'remembering' and the types of experience to be 'remembered' are developed and reinforced through a socialisation process – for instance, parents play a significant role in what is to be considered memorable or unforgettable. Their argument fundamentally considers that memories are very rarely about reporting a mental state or describing an internal process; they are more typically rhetorical, contentious, expressing something of themselves and their position in relation to others around them or the current scheme of things. They are centred on the activities of social life.

For Shotter and Billig (1998), the advocated approach is not so much one of establishing cognitive structure in a psychological sense, but fundamentally one of uncovering the almost unnoticed events and features that exist in social practice. In this construct, it is the unfolding of the activities within which we relate to our surroundings and the responsiveness of ourselves to these features which are key, rather than the idea that there is a form of 'inner landscape' that we come to know. It is in these fleeting, unique discursive activities that we can begin to understand how the unique nature of our inner selves can be expressed to each other. Although I have some affinity with these ideas in a dialogical sense, for I feel that one comes to know through dialogues with the world, I am not entirely sure that discounting the notion of the inner landscape – which I feel Shotter and Billig, as discursive psychologists, do – has validity. Their approach to it is one of cognitive structure rather than metaphorical concept. If we return to Horkheimer and Adorno's (1972) 'getting lost', one can explore getting lost within the physical world, and it is through this getting lost that we come to know more; but one can also explore this getting lost in a psychic sense, where we may no longer see the wood for the trees, or be sure of the right path, or have been this way before – which way did we turn and what was the consequence? An inner geography does not have to be based on cognitive structure, as Shotter and Billig (1998) suggest, but can be considered a metaphorical image of our inner selves.

Finally, and continuing to focus on Shotter and Billig's (1998) work, they recognise that as human beings we cannot remain utterly inert while in the presence of others; nor can we remain entirely detached from our surroundings. As a result, they suggest that we are always in a living relationship of some kind, with others and with the surroundings themselves, and are constantly responsively reshaped by the actions of a second person. It is from this that our actions are a complex mixture of both inner influences and those outside of us. A vital dialogical component, then, is our affective involvement in social practices and our capacity to 'read' the specific variabilities that can occur in both languaged and non-languaged activities with others. Figure 13, above, provides a strong resonance to this phenomenon through its figurative, rather than literal, language.

Much of the issue of language in dialogism and to whom it belongs is covered in Chapter 5, so with this in mind I now turn to how these approaches can be synthesised.

A merging of constructs

My task is to overlay the constructs outlined above so that some sense of order may come out of them which suggests a philosophical basis to a research process. A key theme in both sources of literature is the focus on the unconscious and the conscious. In active imagination's it is the relaxation of the conscious state which allows the unconscious to emerge and enter the conscious. In dialogics the idea is that a consciousness exists in a space between individuals, which is grounded in communication predominantly of a linguistic nature. In active imagination, Samuels (1999) suggests a suspension of ego-control – a dropping down of consciousness to look inwardly – while Nealon (2003) suggests that one must look outwardly to the diversity and risk of the 'other' in order that an adventure of appropriation can occur which enables the confrontation and conquering of new and never-ending forms of otherness. Whilst at first glance these theoretical positions appear as opposites, there is also a sense of commonality, for both inherently suggest the need to lose oneself so that one can be found. Active imagination through the use of imagery provides not only a means of communication, but a method of entering into a process of communication with both self and others. In this sense its application has useful practical qualities.

Once the process of 'losing' and 'finding' oneself is engaged in, then there is the potential for forms of dialogue to emerge. For Bakhtin, the nature of dialogism is a more profound focus than for Jung, where dialogue appears as a more generic term without the same level of rigour. However, Bakhtin uses the terms 'dialogic', 'dialogism' and 'dialogue' in a variety of ways. Whilst dialogics is proposed as having a particular meaning (for instance, multi-voicedness), the other terms appear interchangeably within much of the Bakhtinian texts. What exists in the literature above is the significance of metaphor. In active imagination, symbolism and metaphor exist as the basis for development of self-knowing. In dialogics, the dialogue as multi-voicedness is considered a powerful metaphor in itself, whereby forms of otherness can be considered as non-threatening, and in which voices and responses can occur.

I wish to propose a method whereby the act of symbolic engagement sets out a *dialogical space*. The imaginal object, be it a painting, drawing, music, sculpture or any other medium, is a *form of otherness*. We can assume this if the ego-control has dropped down, for what flows from the unconscious into the conscious had to be considered as 'other', and as we can see from the work produced by the students in this study, not only is that other an internal other, it is grounded archetypally to external forms of otherness. The multi-voicedness is apparent through the personal realisations of experience, professional discourses and social phenomena, and each of these voices places them in some form of personal, professional or social context as the dialogue shifts from the pure 'image' to the critically reflexive commentary upon the image itself. There is also a further element to this – the critique of the work conducted by myself upon it, which is further built on by you, the reader/viewer of both their texts and my own. In this process a clear construct of dialogic intersubjectivity becomes evident. I am in effect an outside voice (as are you), a commentator and a mediator who not only takes these voices as they appear, but creates a textual interplay within them and restructures them as new forms of dialogue.

Methodologically, what is emerging out of this process is the potential to set out a *discursive territory*. To use the quote from Hadjukowski-Ahmed (2003: 355) again: 'Dialogism, which is neither dialogue nor dialectics, is a philosophy of communication that maps the discursive territory of difference.' In a Bakhtinian sense, this discursive territory operates within the construct of social phenomena. However, this notion of difference is in principle not vastly different to the Jungian consideration in therapeutic terms of the uncovering of opposites that exist within the unconscious and the unification of these within ourselves. As Salman (1999) has noted, the relationship between the ego and other elements of the psyche is one of constant dialogue and the nature of the conversation one of constant change. In effect, this discursive territory exists internally, and through the application of active imagination it has the potential to exist externally. A discursive territory can therefore be not only a landscape that explores social relationships, but one which explores the landscape of the psyche. In some ways this is also able to operate at varying levels, for the discursive territory can map out not only these internal conversations, but broader externalised phenomena – for instance, the development of an archetype may also be considered a discursive territory for it maps out what is archetypal from what is different.

Wrapped up in all of these developments is the concept of *betrachten*. The construction of the discursive territory inevitably leads into something else which is not necessarily bounded or the 'finished product'; and, as Jung suggests, the process is not merely to 'look' but to go beyond looking. Let us quickly revisit Jung's statement on this (Jung, 1932, cited in Chodorow, 1997: 3): 'The English verb "to look at" does not convey this meaning, but the German "betrachten", which is an equivalent, means also to make pregnant . . . And if it is pregnant, then something is due to come out of it; it is alive, it produces, it multiplies.' *Betrachten*, in this case, emerges out of what Gurevitch (2003) identifies as plurality in dialogue. Citing Bakhtin (1984), Gurevitch explores the differentiation between dialogue and monologue, and concludes that monologues are closed constructs. Dialogues, on the other hand, are seen by Gurevitch (2003) as mutual projects – common words or texts become shared, and these in turn become unifying topics. These pluralities of dialogue form part of the discursive territory, but they are not bound within it because the territory is not static. The pluralities enliven it, and it is through them that the discursive territory becomes pregnant: The deeper one 'looks', the deeper the conversation; and as a consequence the possibility for multiplication increases.

This is seen by Gurevitch (2003) as problematic, as I noted in Chapter 5 when discussing his idea of the word in language as being half someone else's. This problem is with regard to the communication of intention, for, as he suggests, one must have a sense of owning or acquisition of a language that belongs to oneself. However, whilst I feel that from the perspective of Bakhtin's work this is correct in the scientific method he employs in the study of language, in the approach I am advocating it is vital that the word or symbol *should be* half someone else's (and in this I include the unconscious as a discrete someone as well as another individual), so that the process of *betrachten* is enabled to occur naturally within the discursive territory itself. It is in this process that there exists a transcendent function, where a dialogic threshold is entered into, of self and of other, and where new understandings and questions can be found within this relational space. Gurevitch (2003) suggests that this threshold should be regarded as an actual reality, just as the imaginal psychologists suggest that imagination should be regarded as reality, and reality as imagination. These perspectives add further qualitative layers to the nature of the discursive territory.

Situating the philosophy within an approach to pedagogical application and human inquiry

As yet, I have not come to a model under which these ideas can become a conceptual method that addresses the issues of application to pedagogy, human inquiry, the application of metaphor and transformation. There have been various accounts of theoretical approaches and application to the examples of data itself, but thus far I have not reached a usable and accessible construct, so it is to this that I now turn.

In the first instance, it is perhaps important to remind ourselves of the purpose of such activity as is described above and the outcomes of such experiences. First, with regard to learning, it is predominantly concerned with exploring the nature of critical reflexivity from a number of perspectives, which then leads us into the process of research, but of course it is much deeper than that. Ultimately, the process leads to an exploration of the lived experience and what might be considered essences of reality. It therefore serves two purposes as research methodology, both in the wider public and social domain and in the domain of self as practitioner-researcher:

1   Knowledge production through education and socio-political action.
2   Empowerment through the process of people constructing and using their own knowledge (Winter and Munn-Giddings, 2001).

Whilst at this point I do not want to delve too deeply back into the realms of action research, as I want to propose a different schematic, it is useful to provide an illustration from Carr and Kemmis (1993: 164–5), who cite a definition of 'educational action research' from 1981 outlined at the National Invitational Seminar on Action Research in Geelong, Australia:

> Educational Action Research is a term used to describe a family of activities in curriculum development, professional development, school improvement programmes, and systems planning and policy development. These activities have in common the identification of strategies of planned action which are 'implemented' and then systematically submitted to 'observation', 'reflection', and 'change'. Participants in action being considered are integrally involved in all of these activities.

The key words for me in this passage are *professional development, observation, reflection* and *change*, for the basis of this work lies in these terms.

Now I shall propose a schematic through which the thinking outlined above becomes more clear and accessible. In effect it is a conceptual framework which could be tested out in various learning and research environments.

CONCEPT 1: THE REFLECTIVE REPRODUCTION

The act of utilising the active imagination process through the development of 'images' acts as data collection. The data is in effect both self-generated and self-collected by the individual who engages in the active imagination process. It is in the act of imagining and the construction of the image that the claims and questions resulting out of the reflective reproduction begin to be formulated. As ego-control drops, questions emanate from the unconscious to confront established personal forms of knowing.

CONCEPT 2: IMMERSION IN THE REFLECTIVE REPRODUCTION

In this concept the underlying principle is that imagination may be found in reality, and reality may be found in imagination. Through the developmental process of the forming of the reflective reproduction and the critical commentary, relationships are made between experience and the image as individuals immerse themselves within it and the literature used to explore the emergence of unconscious knowing. In this work the individual chooses their own method of representation, the relationships they find within it situated within their experiences and the literature they have sought out to understand it. In this approach the individual engages in a process of establishing a reality and seeks out an 'other' (such as theoretical models) to establish significance.

CONCEPT 3: ESTABLISHING DIALOGIC POTENTIAL

The reflective reproduction emerges out of the unconscious and becomes located within a space of consciousness upon which it can be worked metaphorically, textually and linguistically. In this work it can be seen at differing levels: first, *reflective reproduction/critical commentary*; second, *submission to a metaphorical analysis*. It is possible that this could progress further, for instance to the development of an archetype – a personification of the image(s). Once each stage has been exhausted, the dialogic potential lies in the increasingly more established collective unconscious and the possibility of it being located more clearly within a social context.

CONCEPT 4: ESTABLISHING A TRANSCENDENT POTENTIAL

In this process there is the submission of ourselves to account; there is no choice, for even if we do not choose to submit something of ourselves, then we have still found out something. In this process individuals may establish 'findings' that are in effect only the beginning of an analytic, the ego may still wish to dominate the decisions over what is and what is not relevant to the process, and indeed the process itself may not be logical or coherent. Once one recognises that, if nothing else, one can change one's own sense of Being, and with it comes the recognition of autonomy and responsibility to one's self; a reflexive ethic.

CONCEPT 5: HEARING AND ORCHESTRATING THE REFLECTIVE VOICES

The author of the reflective reproduction begins to subject the voices within the dialogue to some form of unification (for instance an archetype) in which they are heard singularly and in harmony. They may not be saying the same thing, but placed together they are harmonious, for one can hear them together or pick them out individually. The closest analogy to this is music, where polyphonic voices can be heard across the score. Different instruments play different parts of the score, but they all – even those played in discord – contribute to an overall sound. Voices that are heard to exist in dialogue, both internally and with relationships established with the other, are amplified in the process of analysis.

CONCEPT 6: REFLEXIVE EMERGENCE

In this concept there is a natural process which enables interdependency to occur in the generation of data, in its analysis and as a mechanism for change. Illumination emerges out of the imaginative and dialogic process which triggers an engagement in theoretical bodies of knowledge. Personal experience and understanding are then critiqued from within these bodies of knowledge in the form of a commentary, itself a secondary level of dialogue, and this process is reciprocal as theoretical propositions become questioned by insightful observation of internal sensations and personal meaning. It is in these experiences that transformation begins to occur; or, as Jung (2005) might argue for the case of active imagination, the trigger to individuation.

In summary, I believe this leaves us with a number of concepts consisting of the synthesis of dialogic and active imaginal theories which enable the capture of both personal and professional reflexive spirit and which combine to produce a philosophical approach to engaging in human inquiry. Active imagination provides the means to the establishment of data, while constructs of metaphor and dialogue provide the methods for analysis and understanding at an intensely personal level. By looking – *really looking* – at an experience in this way, a process of *betrachten* occurs. The images become pregnant with multiple possibilities that are not truths in themselves but conjectures upon which further sharing of knowledge can be built.

Conclusion: rupture and transformation

At this point some simple but fundamental questions need to be asked:

1   How and why has this work come about?
2   Who are the researchers?
3   Who and what are transformed?

Hopefully, in the discussions above, I have begun to outline some initial answers to these questions, but as yet I have not placed the construct of this work within some kind of epistemic location. With this in mind, and on reviewing the questions once more, the key term that returns constantly to the dialogue is 'transformation'. Through all of this work I have tried to engage in and develop the mapping out of a discursive territory. From the ideas of space, language, metaphor, dialogics, etc., a discursive territory of *imaginal dialogics* has begun to emerge, both from an educational perspective and as a method of inquiry. It is in this process that some fundamental considerations of subjectivity and objectivity need to be addressed, alongside considerations of aesthetics and methodology.

In order to do this, I would like to concentrate on the thinking of Michel Foucault. In 'Maurice Florence', Foucault (1998a) outlines some of the issues of concern in which the subject himself is proposed as the object of knowledge. In this view, the problem for Foucault (1998a: 459) is 'to determine what the subject must be, to what condition he is subject, what status he must have, what position he must occupy in reality or the imaginary, in order to become a legitimate subject of this or that type of knowledge [*connaissance*]'.

The problem that Foucault (1998b) lays out is one of how something is considered as a possible object of knowledge through a particular set of subjectivications – in other words, considerations of truth exist only within the subjective conditions to which the object has been considered as having potential for knowledge. In the 'game of truth', if one changes the subjective conditions applied to the object, then one changes the potential for knowledge within it. The issue for Foucault (1998a), then, has not been one of truth or verification or how it is constituted, but the various 'truth games' formed through which the subject becomes an object of knowledge. In the first chapter I moved from a history of medicine to an evidence-based medicine, to an evidence-based practice based upon evidence-based medicine. This is a 'truth game', for it is not through a verification of truth and how it is constituted that it has come into being, but through a truth game upon which as a subject it has become an object of knowledge. In application to the self, Foucault (1998a: 461) states it thus:

> Foucault has now undertaken, still within the same general project, to study the constitution of the subject as an object for himself: the formation of procedures by which the subject is led to observe himself, analyse himself, interpret himself, recognize himself as a

domain of possible knowledge. In short, this concerns the history of 'subjectivity', if what is meant by the term is the way in which the subject experiences himself in a game of truth where he relates to himself.

Foucault was of course concerned with much larger considerations, but these kinds of questions still hold up in small-scale work such as this, particularly if we consider his notions of subjectification alongside the questions I ask above. Indeed, they provide us with a foundation for the subjectification process in this kind of work and our own engagement in 'games of truth'.

It is from this that there is increasingly little doubt in my thinking that the reflective reproduction process described above creates a rupture in the notion of knowledge within those who undertake it. The 'catchment area' for this work is mainly those who work in the fields of health, social care and education, as either practitioners or researchers, or both. In the traditional education of these professions knowledge has been seen as coming from external sources, such as literature and empirical research, rather than from within. Indeed, this has been further embedded in practice through clinical governance, evidence-based practice, and ulti- mately proceduralised models of practice delivery grounded in increased levels of policy. In short, practice is governed by what practitioners are told. In learning they are guided into particular forms of socialisation, and they learn the rules of that profession and how to play the game to satisfy those who act as the gatekeepers to it. They are familiar with its territory, and until the point of reaching this form of inquiry all of their practical and academic experiences have been continuous in the methods described above. Suddenly, in this approach, the ground is wrenched from beneath them and they are faced with discontinuity. New modes of learning are employed that mean a change in the rules of the 'truth game'; the usual reference points have disappeared and the learning experiences are threatening, both personally and professionally.

Foucault (2002: 29) suggests that 'once these immediate forms of continuity are suspended, an entire field is set free', and this can be seen both positively and negatively, but it does return us neatly to the question of the production of the work outlined above, and to a deeper, more discursive analysis. This occurs in two separate ways for my purposes. First, there is the suspension of continuity of one mode of practice and the opening up of others as a means to personal knowledge production; and second, there is the opportunity to examine statements that emerge through the methodology and the relationships between them. One can begin to open up and explore the nature of knowledge production more generally from the perspective of different disciplines, opening the fields of the arts and language as valid sources of knowledge within these professions that transgress the traditional forms of empirical texts. This operates at a level which is perhaps aimed more at what constitutes professional ideology rather than that which constitutes professional knowledge, but perhaps it also acts as a mechanism that enables confrontation of professional knowing that gives the individual freedom to engage in the process of active imagination. In this sense there emerge domains in which statements can be proposed and practices established; the first is that of professional ideology, and the second that of personal and professional liberation.

References

Anderson, R. (1998) Intuitive Inquiry. In Baud, W. and Anderson, R., *Transpersonal Research Methods for the Social Sciences*. Sage. London

Bakhtin, M. (1984) *Problems of Dostoevsky's Poetics*. University of Minnesota Press. Minneapolis

Baumann, Z. (1993) *Postmodern Ethics*. Blackwell. Cambridge

Carr, W. and Kemmis, S. (1993) *Becoming Critical: Education, Knowledge, and Action Research*. Falmer Press. Lewes

Chodorow, J. (1997) *C.G. Jung: Jung on Active Imagination*. Routledge. London

Edgar, I. (2004) *Guide to Imagework: Imagination Based Research Methods*. Routledge. London

Fish, D. (1998) *Appreciating Practice in the Caring Professions: Refocusing Professional Development and Practitioner Research*. Butterworth Heineman. Oxford

Folch-Serra, M. (2003) Place, Voice, Space: Mikhail Bakhtin's Dialogical Landscape. In Gardiner, M., *Mikhail Bakhtin*, Vol 4. Sage. London

Foucault, M. (1998a) Maurice Florence. In Fabion, J., *Aesthetics: The Essential Works 2*. Allen Lane/Penguin Press. London

Foucault, M. (1998b) What is an Author? In Fabion, J., *Aesthetics: The Essential Works 2*. Allen Lane/Penguin Press. London

Foucault, M. (2002) *The Archaeology of Knowledge*. Routledge. London

Gurevitch, Z. (2003) Plurality in Dialogue. In Gardiner, M., *Mikhail Bakhtin*, Vol 3. Sage. London

Hadjukowski-Ahmed, M. (2003) Bakhtin without Borders: Participatory Action Research in the Social Sciences. In Gardiner, M., *Mikhail Bakhtin*, Vol 4. Sage. London

Hannah, B. (2001) *Encounters with the Soul: Active Imagination as Developed by C.G. Jung*. Chiron. Wilmette

Hillman, J. (1992) *Revisioning Psychology*. Harper Perennial. New York

Horkheimer, M. and Adorno, T. (1972) *Dialectic of Enlightenment*. Continuum. New York

Johns, C. (2002) *Guided Reflection: Advancing Practice*. Blackwell Science. Oxford

Jung, C. (1932) Interpretation of Visions. Privately mimeographed seminar notes of Mary Foote. 4 May.

Jung, C. (2005) *The Archetypes and the Collective Unconscious* (2nd edn). Routledge. London

McIntosh, P. (2006) Metaphor and Symbolism: An Action Research Approach to Reflexivity in Nurse Education. Unpublished Ph.D. thesis. Centre of Applied Research in Education, University of East Anglia

Nealon, J.T. (2003) The Ethics of Dialogue: Bakhtin and Levinas. In Gardiner, M., *Mikhail Bakhtin*, Vol 4. Sage. London

Salman, S. (1999) The Creative Psyche: Jung's Major Contributions. In Young-Eisendrath, P. and Dawson, T., *The Cambridge Companion to Jung*. Cambridge University Press. Cambridge

Samuels, A. (1999) Jung and the Post-Jungians. In Young-Eisendrath, P. and Dawson, T., *The Cambridge Companion to Jung*. Cambridge University Press. Cambridge

Shotter, J. and Billig, M. (1998) A Bakhtinian Psychology: From Out of the Heads of Individuals and Into the Dialogues between Them. In Mayerfield-Bell, M. and Gardiner, M., *Bakhtin and the Human Sciences*. Sage. London

Shotter, J. and Billig, M. (2003) A Bakhtinian Psychology: From Out of the Heads of Individuals and Into the Dialogues between Them. In Gardiner, M., *Mikhail Bakhtin*, Vol 4. Sage. London

Vannoy Adams, M. (1999) The Archetypal School. In Young-Eisendrath, P. and Dawson, T., *The Cambridge Companion to Jung*. Cambridge University Press. Cambridge

Winter, R. (1989) *Learning from Experience: Principles and Practice in Action Research*. The Falmer Press. Lewes

Winter, R. and Munn-Giddings, C. (2001) *A Handbook for Action Research in Health and Social Care*. Routledge. London

Chapter 7

Concluding thoughts

The linkages to action research and critical creativity

> The semester was coming to an end. What I had read of de Baur and heard him say in the lectures and seminar all fell into place. What we take for reality is merely a text, what we take for texts merely interpretations. Reality and texts are therefore what we make of them.
>
> (Schlink, 2009: 277)

Introduction

My concluding thoughts concern ways that theories and models used in the fields of qualitative research, philosophy, the creative arts and humanities, metaphor and linguistics can be brought together in ways which are purposive, yet at the same time do not have the effect of diluting the rigour and integrity that lie within each of these approaches to interpretation. By 'purposive', I mean that they have significance within the professional fields of health, social care and education as aids to professional development, but also provide ways of inquiring into these fields and the social world so that new insights and propositions for dialogue can be established. I hope that in the preceding work here I have shown that experiential learning, action research and the arts can be brought together and reconstructed in ways for personal and professional knowing which are supported by a range of theoretical frameworks.

There is a painting I often use in my teaching on reflection. It is by Salvador Dali and is called *Painting Gala from the Back*. In this painting, Dali stands at his easel. His back is to the viewer. In front of him sits Gala, his model and long-time companion. She too is only seen from the back. In front of her is a mirror, and in the mirror we see her face and also that of Dali at his canvas.

It is reasonably well known that Dali was interested in science. Some of his most famous paintings are actually representations of quantum physics. He produced *Painting Gala from the Back* twice, with slight variations of tone and angles in the second. At the time this work was produced, in the early 1970s, a photographic technique called 'stereoscopy' was in use, whereby photographs were bounced off a number of mirrors; where they rested on the final mirror, a three-dimensional image appeared. Dali replicated this with his two paintings of Gala, bouncing them off a number of mirrors until a three-dimensional image – a kind of early hologram – appeared to rest on the last mirror.

Bearing in mind my focus on the use of reflection and a range of theories which aid in its effective production, this seems an apt way of constructing the concept of reflection as a three-dimensional process, and also arguing that theories can be used in such ways that they can assist in constructing models which are more than flat, unidimensional propositions. That, to an extent, has been the driver behind all of the writing that precedes this conclusion. However, in order to build such a model, there needs to be scaffolding around it, and that has been provided from two sources: the fields of action research and critical creativity. I want to focus on these two fields now, because their importance – particularly that of critical creativity – has been overshadowed in my writing by the use of metaphor, dialogic and archetypal psychology as 'method', and as a methodologist I feel that I have so far done them a disservice in not sufficiently outlining their importance in this particular work, or to me as an individual engaged in it; for, as you have probably guessed in getting this far, I prefer to work in the margins, where I believe there is real importance. To illustrate this, I want to quote Debbie Horsfall's recollection of a discussion she had with Richard Winter:

> I remember talking with Professor Richard Winter in a lovely coffee shop in Oxford. He has used action research for years. I asked him if he ever got fed up with always having to struggle to justify the type of research methodology he uses. He said no. He felt that if he didn't have to continuously justify, then it would mean that the methodology had become mainstream. If it had become mainstream, then it meant it was no longer challenging the status quo.
>
> (Horsfall and Higgs, 2007: 70)

This is exactly it. This type of work has value precisely because it is not mainstream. If it were, it would have been reduced to a table or a chart, worked through by an application of a methodology deemed satisfactory by the mainstream gatekeepers. I am reminded of a wonderful comment by my good friend and mentor Professor Jack Sanger, which goes something like: 'A quantitative researcher is like a magician. He puts numbers in a hat and pulls out a table.' In effect, this means that such work is constituted of smoke and mirrors. It is not real, it is a deception, for we are deceived into believing what it is that emerges from the statistics and that they apply to all, regardless of culture, gender, social upbringing, values, etc.

Critical creativity, as an antidote to positivism and a welcome addition to interpretivism, enables a challenge to the status quo and supports the development of practice and research in the real world. Its processes are in opposition to those of positivism, for it causes an intellectualising in both the construction of ways to uncover phenomena and the ways in which phenomena become uncovered. You cannot simply put this work into an Excel spreadsheet and expect the results of the data merely to pop out (although no doubt someone will try!). It also does not shy away from the relationship between the researcher and the subjects or objects of the research, and it is transparent in direct opposition to the way in which positivism obfuscates its role in the process – being reflexive is a reflexive way of being, we cannot escape from it or hide it, it is in all of us to greater or lesser extents, it is just that critically creative researchers have harnessed its potential and opened themselves to it. As such, I feel it is necessary to include some of my own reflections in being exposed to some of the work produced by the students in the previous chapters:

> For me this work has been one of emergence, where I have come to know something about myself in the process of coming to know something about others. I have met people through this work, both in literature and in life, who have helped me to come to know these things, or have triggered a process of self-realisation. It is a strange feeling when someone points something out to you about yourself which you were previously unaware of which is so spookily accurate that it makes the hair on the back of your neck stand on end. This has occurred for me both in direct conversations and through the ghosts found in the texts of my reading . . .

> In my various 'roles' of father, husband, son, lecturer, etc., the relationship that I have with my ego has begun to be uppermost in my considerations. No more importantly has this been felt than in my role as 'researcher', for I have had to manage the challenge of this whole process as an adult when in my mind I'm still 'little Paul McIntosh – Eric's lad'.

> (McIntosh, 2006: 431–3)

Ian Percy (2007: 97) provides a way of describing this kind of experience, by suggesting that 'this creation of personal narratives influences the formation of the storyteller's possible identities while, at the same time, these identities shape the telling of their personal narratives'. In my own reflexive account I ask questions in relation to this particular phenomenon, and make some conclusions on it:

> Why should I be telling you this? Or why do I even recount it? This is quite simple; these memories and images were evoked in me when I began to engage in the portfolios presented here by the participants. It was then that I began to look – really look – at what lies within them with regard to the ego that the remembrances occurred. I suppose what I am trying to say, and what I am beginning to understand, is how internally we are shaped by the external other, and that once there in the psyche, these things are pretty much there for good.
>
> (McIntosh, 2006: 434)

As well as the reflexive basis to this discussion, I feel if I am to align my work with a particular approach, then it needs to be one which is broad and flexible enough to accommodate my own thinking. The writing of Brendan McCormack and Angie Titchen (2007) enables this kind of alignment without being prescriptive. In their chapter 'Critical Creativity: Melding, Exploding, Blending' they situate their ideas within the *critical paradigm*, which is informed from a number of perspectives, such as creative development, research, education and practice, but also recognise that there is more to practical wisdom than the simple application of abstract theory, for there is a requirement for skills, sensitivities and capacity to engage in practical activity. For McCormack and Titchen (2007: 43), practical activity is 'a form of praxis in which practitioners learn how to pick out salient features of their environment, develop perspicuous responses to those features, and adjust and adapt themselves to the particularities of a given situation'.

In this sense, as they point out, there is a need and vitality in synergistic use of conceptual, theoretical and methodological advances which enable emancipatory professional development and sustainable change – particularly when grounded in action research ideals. Usefully, what McCormack and Titchen work through is the progression from one paradigmatic synthesis into another – first, the application of artwork to engage in questions of practice development (critical creativity), and, second, application of the outcomes of these to an emancipatory form of inquiry, which eventually leads to a series of assumptions about such work. I have abbreviated these below.

Philosophical

1   There is a creative connection and blending of assumptions, if assumptions across different development and research paradigms are combined within a project.
2   Creative expression creates synergy between cognitive and artistic approaches to critique.
3   Transformational development and research are person centred.
4   The three philosophical approaches above are blended with spiritual intelligence.

Theoretical

1   There is a movement from conscious to unconscious blending of assumptions.
2   World views are connected through the honouring of commonalities and traditions.
3   Human flourishing is an intentional means as well as the ultimate end.
4   Human becoming through critically creative learning and facilitation.

Methodological

It is assumed that a critically creative approach to reflective action is the key methodological approach, and that the power to blend the philosophical and theoretical assumptions and convert them into action, transformational development and research emerge from professional artistry. Although professional artistry is not unique to critical creativity, its critically creative approach to reflective action is, and so its approach has the following concerns:

- Learning through intellectual, aesthetic and expressive creativity.
- Releasing energy for creative practice through the use of creative arts media and intellectually creative thinking and problem-solving.
- Practising creatively as a practitioner, facilitator/educator, developer or researcher.

(McCormack and Titchen, 2007: 48–52)

Both mine and McCormack and Titchen's frameworks are therefore embedded with creativity as forms of enablement for transformative action and as professional artistry which open up the possibility of human flourishing through different forms of inquiry – either as methodologically rigorous as research, facilitated process, or as informal and flexible practitioner-researcher reflection. The frameworks are not prescriptive, but exemplars of the forms they can take. Indeed, it could be argued that my work is an exemplar of the assumptions outlined by McCormack and Titchen – a working example of a wider set of principles which can be read and applied in a range of ways.

Re-imaging through action research

From this point, it is perhaps most important that we establish exactly what action research is *not*. It is not a bounded methodology, tied up in forms of rule and regulation in its application. It is not a form of inquiry that insists upon hierarchy, defining who is the researcher and who are the subjects. It is not an approach that is necessarily led by an academic vanguard who decides what will be researched. As we saw in Chapter 2, action research can be about individual practice improvement, organisational development, liberation, equity and self-reliance. Equally, it can exist within the scholarly tradition of knowledge generation (Reason and Bradbury, 2008) through small-scale face-to-face inquiry and in larger scales in areas such as social policy. This is its beauty and elegance, for it transgresses policy, professional, organisational and personal boundaries in ways that other forms of inquiry do not; and because it sees its primary role as one of social justice and confrontation of the status quo, it is not afraid to embrace disparate ways of doing so. Its members may argue about how these approaches contribute to it, but there is still an underlying value shared in its exuberance and diversity, and in its incitement to dialogue (Reason and Bradbury, 2008). Further, its purpose is 'to contribute to the onging revisioning of the Western mindset – to add impetus to the movement away from a modernist worldview based on a positivist philosophy and values system dominated by crude notions of economic progress, toward emerging perspectives which share a "postmodern" sentiment (in the widest sense of that term)' (Reason and Bradbury, 2008: xxiii). This is not just elegant but essential, for societies cannot exist solely on a financial model of economic capital, which is ascribed to through current positivist thinking. It also needs a human and spiritual model of social capital, for the problems of the modern world cannot be solved by money and technology alone.

When re-imagining action research in the way that I perceive it, I feel it is important to focus on some of the key concepts of action research and the ways in which 'imagining' or 'imaging' can be utilised within it. For me, one of the most fundamental of these concepts is 'liberation'. This can be explored sociologically – as a form of participatory action research in the way that Fals Borda (2008) constructs it, through challenges to value-neutrality and aloofness in relation to scientific constructions of social theory – or as a form of personal inquiry through which new and personal knowing 'authors' an individual liberation from that which has created boundedness in action and thinking. As a mode of inquiry, this re-imagining action in the action research process or as a mode of critical creativity must always have as its basis the value of spirituality. James Hillman (1992: vii), quoting Yeats' 'Sailing to Byzantium', typifies what I mean by this. The soul becomes both the student and the object of study, not in a cognitive sense, but as a state of being:

> . . . man is but a paltry thing,
> A tattered coat upon a stick, unless
> Soul clap its hands and sing, and louder sing
> For every tatter in its mortal dress,
> Nor is there singing school but studying
> Monuments of its own magnificence . . .

The spiritual is not necessarily constructed within the confines of religion, for its application and significance spread much wider than that. Constructing ways through action research, creativity and the imagination is, as Yeats' words suggest, a celebration of the human condition in ways which do not deride or repress as the current forms of technical rationalism do. Action research and critical creativity facilitate growth through their various forms. Technical rationalism limits, confines, blocks human growth and flourishing. Its intentions are to repress, and it does so with great efficiency, as Robert Flood (2008: 127) notes:

> [S]eeking absolute mastery over our lives, as science and technology do, misses the point of wholeness and takes away our human spirit. It turns the magic of mystery in our lives into the misery of failed mastery over our lives . . . Such recognition spotlights the futility, let alone the hostility, of traditional forms of practice based on prediction and control, which are so prominent in today's social organizational arrangements. It is futile because any social dynamic will always remain beyond control. It is hostile because it attacks people's spiritual well-being by isolating us and treating us as separate objects rather than

appreciating patterns of relationship that join us together in one dynamic.

A resonant discussion of the application of humanistic approaches is provided by John Rowan (2008). In this, he observes that the work of humanistic psychology has enabled a view of research which is grounded in the notion of treating people as if they are human. He suggests that in this process we, as researchers, take up a critical role. Reflexivity needs to be taken seriously, for we may find that what is uncovered in the research may also apply to ourselves, and we should resist any urge to be alienated from it, or exclude ourselves from it. Whilst Rowan argues that quantitative research has a place, it should be considered when the evidence of qualitative research applied prior to it enables knowledge of what it means when it is carried out. Finally, it is the self and other, as previously discussed, which are central to the process. Citing the work of Michelle Fine (1994), Rowan argues that the concept of 'Real Self' acts as a point of reference from which authenticity of the research findings and process can be understood. Essentially, an expression of a humanistic value system and the roots through which it is nourished provide these points of authenticity. Whether this operates through quantitative or qualitative methodologies is, to an extent, irrelevant, for either should have at its core the recognition that both the researched upon and the researchers are people and are human. This, of course, matters in all forms of research, but it has particular importance in both action research and critical creativity. As Edgar Schein (2008: 194) concludes:

> We have to understand better the consequences of different forms of intervention and to make sure that our research process does not unwittingly harm our subjects and/or clients.

> My feeling when I look at journals . . . is that the positivistic research paradigm is imperialistic, yet has shown itself all too often to be an emperor with no clothes. It is time to try something new. And that something new . . . Isn't it more important to try and help [them] and learn in the process than to make a sacred cow out of a research paradigm that produces neither valid knowledge nor help.

Finally, on the subject of the limitations of positivism as human exploration and development, and as a mechanism for change, I turn to the words of William Passmore (2008: 46):

When action research, organization development, or participative methods of community development are invoked, they almost always face scepticism, despite their impressive record of success. More often than not we continue to witness change driven from the top down, by the few with the power to control the many, without regard to the potential benefits of greater involvement by those who must implement the new way of operating. We continue to see failed efforts to improve organizational performance or community well-being followed not by efforts to involve people in learning what went wrong but instead by replacing leaders with others who repeat the same process over and over again.

It is interesting that, as Passmore points out, the results of action research are not 'marginal' but significant. And yet action research remains in the margins, as Richard Winter (1989) states, as a form of resistance to the dominant paradigm. In my view, action research is not only a form of resistance and a catalyst for change and social justice; it also enables individuals to exercise latent potential for creativity. It does not try to create conformity; it allows space for what it means to be human, which when combined with, or used alongside, critical creativity opens up possibilities of individuation rather than confines them as a means of control. When I talk of re-imagining action research, I am referring to the values which underpin action research, some of which I have begun to outline above, applied to forms of creative imagination and expression through which a number of outcomes may emerge:

1   Participants are energised by the opportunity to be creative.
2   Critically creative spaces open up for dialogue.
3   Creative pauses emerge for critical thinking.
4   There is a regaining of spirit and collaboration.
5   The voices of those most dismissed are heard through imagining.
6   What is imagined becomes real to others, which in turn creates new realities for others.
7   There is increased understanding of the 'Real Self'.
8   Through imagining, people can author personal and social change.

In so doing, forms of research and professional development artistry can permeate through action. The action of engaging in creativity, such as the arts or humanities, enables forms of observation and questioning which could never emerge out of other forms of inquiry or practice. In them lies the capacity for thinking more like an artist, as Della Fish (1998) suggests, broadening a way of looking – *really looking* – beyond the surface to that which lies beneath.

In all this work so far I have cited others. I have critiqued their work and commented on it from my own inherently biased view. I have acted as a researcher, and commented on the work of 'my' students. And yet, other than this commentary, I have provided nothing of my own 'creation', as such. Although I trained as an artist in my youth, in my own work now I am more attracted to the written and spoken word as my own forms of creative outlet. Below is a piece of my creative writing – a short extract from something much longer – which I hope provides some representation of entering into a critically creative space:

Henry and Jean's clothes hung over an airer above the stove in her kitchen. She had found him an old dressing gown and some paint-spattered jogging bottoms to wear that she used when she decorated. They finished a good six inches above his ankles and when he emerged from the bedroom, looking like a transvestite who had recently competed in an Olympic door-frame painting event, she mockingly announced him as 'Doctor Henry James, internationally renowned scholar of Greek mythology' to the imaginary guests in her living room.

Henry took a generously portioned glass of whisky from her hand.

'Perhaps I'll send a photo of myself dressed like this back to the university.'

'You'll only confirm to them that they dumped you just in time, before you went completely bonkers.'

He sat back in his chair and took a large gulp of his drink, tracing its warmth as it spread down his throat and into his stomach, and looked seriously across to Jean.

'No, being there was bonkers. I had no life Jean, no identity. I was defined as an academic – I defined myself as an academic, it was what I did, it was . . . it was all that I was, I'm beginning to see that now. All those years of research and writing to build up an academic profile – an international reputation for what? – for some bloody student to finish up raving at you for referring their mid-term paper. Apparently when you pay your tuition fees now you are paying for your degree parchment and no longer need to work for it, such is the power of education as a commodity in this modern world. The customer is always right, don't you know? No. I'm very glad I'm out, the outside world is so much saner.'

'It's funny,' replied Jean, 'I often think of this world as an insane one – I mean, look at us, scratching out a living in some desolate corner of the world. This is no idyll, Henry. When the sun's out it's God's own country, but after a few weeks of drizzle and darkness it's easy to become depressed. Yet we've chosen to be here – that's a kind of madness, isn't it?'

I will leave you, the reader, to draw your own conclusions and interpretations on this, but what I have attempted to do is develop a piece of writing which provides a narrative based on observations from real life: the things we see, hear and *feel*. It is an intellectualisation of an experience, explored through figurative, rather than literal, language which opens us up in some small way to an example of the human condition – questions of identity, place, purpose, vocation and the relationships with others that are perceived to exist across all of these various questions. For how we are and how we are perceived to be are by no means the same; and how we understand ourselves to be and how we really are, again, are different. Yet, although it is unlikely that we will fully know ourselves in life, we can come to know aspects of ourselves through sketching out images and literature as a form of critical reflection. For Henry, in the extract above, it is only through moving 'outside' what is known that he begins to see the reality of being 'inside' as he knew it.

Conclusion

With regard to both the pedagogical and research applications of the ideas that litter this book, I am becoming a little clearer, though I am still to an extent unsure of what occurs within the classroom and research settings that enables people to write and create with the freedom that has been displayed in the figures presented here. And although some of my work has concentrated on a pedagogic process, as teaching, learning and practice development, I am beginning to wonder whether it has anything to do with what goes on in these settings at all, or whether it has to do with all the factors that happen *outside* of them – the thorny issues that confront practitioners as people and professionals in their practice – which are largely out of their control. Perhaps the classroom and research forums have offered havens which they have come to periodically from their shark-infested waters to produce such work. Does the work presented here constitute 'evidence'? In my view it most certainly does, but of a different nature: that of the human condition – of normal responses to both ordinary and extraordinary events. It does not need quantifying or pathologising as we appear so keen to do through our desires for absolute truths and professional power games in the current social and professional climate. It simply requires to be heard and to be seen. What we glean from it may be different to the reason for its being, but that is no bad thing, for it opens up the infinite possibilities of its interpretation from our own unique lens on the world.

The work presented in this study is a very small sample of what I have been privileged to view and read in the last few years. Close to a hundred students have now produced reflective portfolios and critical commentaries of various sorts, some of them simply stunning but not necessarily practical for the purposes of this book. In this work I have been anxious to do justice to their commitment, ingenuity and talent, particularly those who have trusted me with their work in the production of this text. I hope I have repaid their trust in me through doing the best possible job I could.

I wish to finish with a note of spirituality. In this final piece I have begun to suggest that through action research and critical creativity we can engage in forms of spirituality that we did not know existed within us. Increasingly, my appreciation of my world is one of psychogeography – locating my feelings, thoughts and understanding of the world through places that are grounded in physical geography, nature and open space, and applying my knowledge and learning to those mental and open spaces. (W.G. Sebald (2002) provides a wonderful example of such appreciation in his book *The Rings of Saturn*.)

To illustrate this, I want to describe a scene to you:

Three coaches sit parked by a wall that runs alongside the quay. Its inhabitants have departed and now stand patiently as the ferry lowers its ramp. From the funnel of the ferryboat a wisp of diesel smoke drifts across the small harbour and into the steel blue sky reflected in and inseparable from the water beneath. Below the surface the jade greens of the seaweed and the white sand of the sea bed can be seen, such is the translucence of the water.

We board the ferry with the coach visitors and make our way across the small channel to the island, curving through the sand banks that lay reassuringly but menacingly below the boat and in a matter of minutes are at the slipway, the small village and its cottages sheltering us from the wind. I am walking more slowly now. The people disperse and within a few short minutes I am on my own. There are no man-made sounds: no engines, no radios, no aircraft, no voices. There is only the sound of the wind – constant and wild – and the sea.

Walking through scrubland, I come to a beach. The sand is white and smooth. Small granite rocks grow out of it closer to the water, greys, greens and blues merge into one another on their rough surfaces. I huddle behind one to shelter myself from the wind. The sun is bright, the sky vibrant blue and the occasional cloud passes quickly over, but it is cold: cold enough to freeze my ears and fingers. I pull my hat over my ears and push my hands into my pockets.

I look back across the sound over which I have just sailed, the Sound of Iona, to Fionnphort, its harbour and its pink granite cliffs. I could, given the clarity of the sea and the white sand, be in the Caribbean, but the wind blowing in off the Atlantic tells me I am not. I am on the Isle of Iona, regarded as the cradle of Christianity, looking back towards the Isle of Mull off the west coast of Scotland.

When I step onto the Isle of Iona I feel different. Although it is regarded as the place where St Columba built his monastery, and still has a substantial Christian community that works hard to maintain its abbey and its ideals, it is not a religious feeling that I experience, for I have no particular religious beliefs. It is much more spiritual. It is where I feel connected to the world and feel authentic. It is not a feeling of yearning for a fantasy way of life, for life can be harsh there in winter (some years ago a group of young men were travelling back to Iona across the Sound following a party on Mull when their boat overturned in rough sea and all were lost – virtually the whole population of the island's young men was wiped out), it is more one of just being in the 'right place'. It is a place for thinking and reflecting.

It was when looking back across the channel towards Fionnphort from Iona that the ideas that form the basis of this book came to me. The space allows me to think and act creatively, and it is where I feel most human. I return constantly to these islands and find something that I cannot find elsewhere, and it is the place where my own writing about Henry and Jean is situated. It is both real and acts as a metaphor for a place where I wish to be that transgresses my physical and psychological senses of being. In my own way, I understand this as archetypal, for it is the combination and connections of the water, the sky and the land as properties which nourish, heal and energise inquiry. The landscape speaks to me, as Yi-Fu Tuan (2003) would say, and now I am going to watch the sun go down over it.

References

Fals Borda, O. (2008) Participatory (Action) Research in Social Theory: Origins and Challenges. In Reason, P. and Bradbury, H., *Handbook of Action Research*. Sage. London

Fine, M. (1994) Working the Hyphens: Reinventing Self and Other in

Qualitative Research. In Denzin, N.K. and Lincoln, Y.S., *Handbook of Qualitative Research*. Sage. Thousand Oaks

Fish, D. (1998) *Appreciating Art in the Caring Professions: Refocusing Professional Development and Practitioner Research*. Butterworth Heinemann. Oxford

Flood, R. (2008) The Relationship of 'Systems Thinking' to Action Research. In Reason, P. and Bradbury, H., *Handbook of Action Research*. Sage. London

Higgs, J., Titchen, A., Horsfall, D. and Armstrong, H. (2007) *Being Critical and Creative in Qualitative Research*. Hampden Press. Sydney

Hillman, J. (1992) *Re-visioning Psychology*. Harper Perennial. London

Horsfall, D. and Higgs, J. (2007) Boundary Riding. In Higgs, J., Titchen, A., Horsfall, D. and Armstrong, H., *Being Critical and Creative in Qualitative Research*. Hampden Press. Sydney

McCormack, B. and Titchen, A. (2007) Critical Creativity: Melding, Exploding, Blending. In Higgs, J., Titchen, A., Horsfall, D. and Armstrong, H., *Being Critical and Creative in Qualitative Research*. Hampden Press. Sydney

McIntosh, P. (2006) Metaphor and Symbolism: An Action Research Approach to Reflexivity in Nurse Education. Unpublished Ph.D. thesis. Centre of Applied Research in Education, University of East Anglia

Passmore, W. (2008) Action Research in the Workplace: The Socio-technical Perspective. In Reason, P. and Bradbury, H., *Handbook of Action Research*. Sage. London

Percy, I. (2007) Living Reflexive Qualitative Research: Resonance and Authenticity. In Higgs, J., Titchen, A., Horsfall, D. and Armstrong, H., *Being Critical and Creative in Qualitative Research*. Hampden Press. Sydney

Reason, P. and Bradbury, H. (2008) *Handbook of Action Research*. Sage. London

Rowan, J. (2008) The Humanistic Approach to Action Research. In Reason, P. and Bradbury, H., *Handbook of Action Research*. Sage. London

Schein, E. (2008) Clinical Inquiry/Research. In Reason, P. and Bradbury, H., *Handbook of Action Research*. Sage. London

Schlink, B. (2009) *Homecoming*. Phoenix. London

Sebald, W.G. (2002) *The Rings of Saturn*. Vintage. London

Tuan, Y.F. (2003) *Space and Place: The Perspective of Experience*. University of Minnesota Press. Minneapolis

Winter, R. (1989) *Learning from Experience: Principles and Practice in Action Research*. The Falmer Press. Lewes

Index